DEBBIE BEHAN

The Adventures of

Bray and Zac

The Magic Portal

The Adventures of Bray and Zac - The Magic Portal

Published in 2016 by Little Butterfly Books
Revised with subtitle (previously Chariot and Planets)

Copyright © 2014 Debbie Behan

Book Cover Design by Little Butterfly Books

Images copyright: Shutterstock
Bladerunner Font- copyright 2002 by Phil Steinschneider

Editor Sally Odgers - Affordable Manuscripts

All rights reserved.

These stories are works of fiction. Names, characters, places, and incidents are either products of the author's imagination or used fictitiously. Any resemblance to actual events, locales, or persons, living or dead, is entirely coincidental.

No part of this publication may be reproduced, stored in a retreval system or transmitted in any form by any means without the prior written permission of the publishers and copyright owners.

A record of this title has been registered at the National Library of Australia

The Adventures of Bray and Zac - The Magic Portal by Debbie Behan

ISBN - Paperback - 978-0-9874013-7-3
ISBN - EBook - 978-0-9874013-0-4

Dedicated to my grandsons

~ Kai and Josh ~

for giving me the inspiration for this space adventure

Chapter One

Project Eight

Bray got home from school; cross he had to work on his new project on his own. His best buddy, Zac, was caught name calling and had detention. In his room, Bray, tossed himself on the bed, muttering, 'To hell with the stupid planets.' He punched the pillow.

'You okay son?' His stepdad popped his head in. 'You got troubles?'

'What do you care? Go find Mum and annoy her.' Bray couldn't stand his new stepdad. 'What a jerk,' he said quietly after he left him alone.

Bray woke an hour later to his mum calling him for dinner. He had a huge size chip on his shoulder because his mum got married before he had even met the man. He hated him for no other reason than he now had to share his mum. *Loser new dad,* he grumbled as he joined them for dinner, but only to irritate them. He had a burger on the way home and wasn't the least bit hungry.

As he pushed his mash around the plate he eyed his mum. 'So, you two met in the casino and after one weekend got married. How's that working out for you?' His voice was almost evil because he was still so cross. He didn't imagine his mum would be so spontaneous. Marry a man she only just met? Bray was smart, the top of his class, but he didn't see that coming.

His mum put her knife and fork down with a clunk. 'Bray! That's enough. It's been a month. Eishol is my husband now. We love each other. Please give him a go or at least try to be polite. For me — please!'

She had put on the waterworks this time. It boiled Bray's temper. 'I'll give it a rest when you kick him out. I'm the man of the house. You said so. Now you say he is. Well... well, have him.' Frustration flowed. Heated tears ran down his cheeks. 'I hate you and I hate him.' He ran back to his room, angry that he had made his mum cry... again! Why he added that he hated her he didn't know. That was so not the truth.

When she called in on him an hour later it was dark in his room. She stood in the light not saying anything.

The Magic Portal

'Sorry Mum. You know I didn't mean what I said about you.'

'I know sweetheart. But please try to give our new family a go. I promise. No more surprises.'

'I'll try,' was all he could muster.

The whole thing had been one big drain on his strength. He sighed and rolled away from the light. His red curls were stuck to his forehead from sweating in anger. With his hand shaking a little, he smoothed his hair back off his face. He was one of the smallest kids in his class, but what he didn't have in size he had in guts. Tonight he overdid it, but being twelve years old he had no idea how to handle the anger he felt towards them now for having to share his mum. He pondered but soon switched back to his project. Now he felt more himself, he again looked forward to starting the solar system he and Zac planned to make using papier-mâché.

An hour later when sleep still hadn't come to relieve his worries, he threw back the covers. In bare feet he padded across the floor to his desk, found the cord to the lamp and switched it on. The room lit up. Pressing his nose to the glass he squinted to see outside. It was then he saw a light on across the street.

'Zac's light is on. Yes!' Bray cheered quietly. He had sulked and had put himself to bed early. It

Adventures of Bray and Zac

was only eight o'clock. He picked up his two-way. 'Hey Zac, you awake?'

He heard a crackle and muffled sound.

'Cripes you frightened the bee geezers out of me. I was going to call you up earlier to talk to you about that library book we borrowed, but I saw your light off and thought you were either asleep or playing happy families and watching a movie with your olds,' said Zac, 'so I thought I better not intrude.'

'Pff, you're kidding me right. Happy family we are not. And as for, *him*, it's his fault my mum is cranky at me! So I was ticked off and went to bed early, but that's not why I can't sleep. I keep thinking about this project. And what did you say about a library book? Didn't catch what you said.' Bray peered out his bedroom door to make sure his mum and Eishol were busy watching television. He heard a movie playing so he knew they were.

Zac said, 'Come over and I'll show you something strange. Maybe after, we can start work on the space project tonight. I'm not sleepy either.'

'What about the stuff we were going to get? Can't believe you ended up in detention. I told you not to fight my battles and to leave Grogan to me. He is one big bully and I am so sick of him,' Bray said.

The Magic Portal

Zac huffed. 'All I did was to call him a sissy, not loud enough for him to hear. Only the teacher overheard me say it. I had to write fifty times on the board, *do not call boys a sissy.*'

'Geez, Grogan would have knocked you into tomorrow if he *had* heard it.' Bray was worried for him.

'Whatever. Look, are we chatting all night on this thing or are you coming over? I've got everything we need; I really want to work on something other than a blackboard,' he joked to let Bray know he wasn't cross. He just hated talking about Grogan, the biggest idiot in their class.

'Coming.' Bray switched off his hand piece.

Bray was looking forward to starting the assignment. It was a cool night so he slipped on sweat pants, a t-shirt, runners and a jacket. Hurrying, he tossed his notes from the desk into his backpack and slung it over his shoulders. As he lifted his window and jumped from it to the ground, he was glad he decided to wear long pants and shoes. He landed on the rose bush which would have really scratched up bare legs and feet.

Across the road he scurried to Zac's place, where Zac met Bray at the door. 'Mum and Dad are at a work function, and sis is out the back with her boyfriend so we are free to make as much noise as

Adventures of Bray and Zac

we want.' He gave a braces-glinting grin.

The mouth hardware was new and Bray felt for him. Not only had he seen how self-conscious Zac was at school, but he'd said they felt nasty in his mouth. Around him, though, Zac didn't care and Bray was glad. He liked the way he smiled.

Bray had a big gap in his front teeth and wished his mum had the money to fix this. They had food in the cupboard and his shoes didn't have holes in them, so they weren't poor; just not as wealthy as Zac's parents. Bray remembered a time when Zac's mum didn't work. That was a long time ago. Bray much preferred to have less and have his mum there when he come home from school than to be wealthy and have her never be there at all. Things had sure changed for Zac. But still, he was going to have the coolest teeth in college.

Bray had to look up as Zac was a good head taller than him. His dark-brown hair and eyes made his skin pale in the moonlight.

'What's going on? Are you sick? You're as white as a ghost.' Bray slid his glasses down so he could see his friend better.

'Well, as I said, I've got something to show you. Something strange is going on in my room. Started an hour ago when I tried to undo that book we borrowed from the library.' Zac urged him to follow.

'What, the leather-bound one with the locking gear? Thought the librarian said it wasn't locked. I mean, we only wanted it so we could get the mythology connected to the planets. If it's useless we can google it. Just thought it might give us a heads up on all the other students, 'cos they'll all be googling,' Bray said. He climbed the stairs behind Zac with gusto. This was what he liked more than anything; *a good challenge.*

'I know.' Zac turned and waited for him. He had long legs and tackled the stairs easily, three at a time. 'It was a great idea to get some ancient symbols to add to our planets after we make them. But the book seriously creeps me out. It's making whispery sounds like horses and smells funny… more like a phone app than a book.' He flung his door open and paused to sniff. 'It's worse.' Zac gulped audibly.

The entire bedroom was full of mist. There seemed to be a strong wind swirling and no sooner had Bray noticed it, than they were sucked into the room, and the door slammed loudly behind them. In fact the vacuum was so strong both boys landed on the floor, one each side of the book.

'You left it on the floor?' Bray rubbed his hip where he landed hard.

'No! It was on my desk. Don't ask me how

it got on the floor and opened its own lock.' Zac looked scared. His head moved from side to side, looking to see if someone was playing a trick on them. 'There has to be someone here!' he whispered in a strained voice. 'Sis? You messing me about?'

There was a loud clap and a hole formed within the pages of the book. As it got larger, both boys seemed to swirl in a circle. They watched each other go out of shape as if they had no bones, just a melted body, and opened their mouths in a shared scream. Around and around they went until their bodies disappeared into what they thought looked like a portal that had opened up within the leather binding of the library book.

Still screaming and not knowing what futuristic hell they had just discovered, they grabbed for each other and held on for grim death.

Chapter Two

Chariot

Their screams were muffled by the sound of horses racing.

BANG! THUD!

Both of them landed.

'Where are we?' Zac stared at Bray, too frightened to look.

They both felt their bodies, glad they seemed normal again. Whatever they had landed on jolted and wheeled; feeling like a billy kart out of control.

Bray looked up and saw a man cracking a whip in the air and shouting at horses in front of him. He could see they were in a cart, and that it was attached to the horses too. Looking around him he identified it as some sort of chariot that the horses pulled. Unbelievable!

Bray looked behind them. A planet or star or something very bright followed them. It was as if the horses dragged it as well. Bray blinked furiously as he tried to erase the thought that popped into his head. *No.*

Zac had hold of his arm tightly, not game to look around at what was putting that fear in his friend's eyes. He gulped back the need to throw up. Finally he did look because Bray kept silent and looked dumbstruck. What he did see was as much as he could take. The horrid vision of Bray turning into spaghetti to fit into the book and now this… he turned his head to the side and let his dinner hurl out into the sky. It sat still, clumps of food and liquid not moving from where he was sick. The only movement was them and the beasts that pulled the chariot.

'Look, no gravity up here to move my spew.' He wiped his mouth.

Bray pulled him back towards him. 'Where are we? This is a dream for sure. Maybe I'm still home and didn't come over at all. I think I'm still sleeping and dragged you into this nightmare. Sorry Zac.'

'Or maybe it's my dream, whatever, wake-the-hell-up!' Zac slapped his face then Bray's.

'What was that for? It's not going to wake

me up if I'm in my own bed.' Bray rubbed at his stinging cheek.'

The man driving the horses swung around. 'Quit it you two. We're nearly there.'

Dumbfounded, they sat quiet as ordered.

'Get a move on!' He cracked the whip. 'Light is fading!' The man's loud voice yelled at the horses and had Bray and Zac looked for a way to get off. Neither understood how the sun or whatever it was following them gave off no heat.

Bray slapped a hand to his head. 'I think...' He swallowed. What he thought seemed preposterous.

'What?' prompted Zac.

'I think that man is Helios, the sun god.'

'What!' Zac frowned at him. 'You're joking, right?'

'Well, we were just sucked through a book into a chariot out in space...'

'But Helios? He was described as handsome, a god who wore a crown that glowed like the sun.' Zac strained his neck and squinted to see the charioteer better. 'Let me tell you, this guy looks like an old man from my angle. No way under all that hair blowing around could I imagine anyone calling him handsome? And where is his crown?'

'Shush! He'll hear you! *Whisper.*' Bray thought Zac sounded hysterical and moved closer to him. 'You're right, but we learned about him in school. He has to be the god who drove the chariot dragging the sun across the sky each day, returning to the east at night. By the position of the Milky Way, we are heading east.'

Zac stuck his head up to see how many horses pulled the chariot. 'Well if you are right, I wonder which one is which. What were the horses names again?'

Bray removed his glasses and cleaned them on his t-shirt. 'They were given fiery names, remember: Pyrios, Aeos, Aethon and Phlegon.'

'That's right. But where is Helios's crown? If this *is* him?' Zac picked at his nose, his forehead wrinkled in thought.

Bray slapped his hand. 'Zac stop it. Every time you get nervous you end up with a sore in your nose and look like you have boogers there. This has to be a dream. Just play it out calmly. We'll wake up soon. I know we will. This isn't possible.'

Suddenly the horses and chariot skidded to a stop. The night sky was in darkness except for the dim light of the moon and stars up above; so many of them. Bray was about to comment on the amazing sight when Helios turned. As he did, a crown magically appeared on his head. It lit up their surroundings. The god was not blurred from the speed they travelled now and they could see him better. He had on a white toga with a thick golden sash that held the material around him. His bulging muscles were clearly visible on one arm. Both boys cringed together until he spoke. Surprisingly, his voice was almost musical and calm.

'Sorry boys, you arrived a bit sooner than I expected. Thought I had time to finish for the day before your curiosity began tampering with the book.'

'Is that how you think we got here?' Bray pinched his eyebrows together in temper. 'I think this is just a dream and I want you to take me and Zac home, now.'

'Come on my boy! Where's your adventurous side gone? Follow me and we'll talk.' He stepped out of the chariot onto the greenest grass they had seen. 'Come. I don't bite.'

Both boys jumped up but not because they wanted to follow. There were funny shaped humans with huge heads and horns heading towards them. No way were they staying there alone.

The horned half-men-half-bulls-in-suits passed them and began tending to the horses.

'Come on Zac!' Bray whispered. 'I'd sooner stay with the god. He can get us home. I know he can. We just have to see what he wants and why we are here.'

'I've got a better idea. Let's use this time with this god because even if it is a dream, we are here and so is he. We may be able to find out more about the planets that none of our school friends would know.'

They high five each other. 'Yes! Let's do it ... Top marks all the way on this one.'

Bray grinned as they ran after Helios. 'Wait up Helios. You are Helios, right?'

'Yes!' called Helios without looking back.

'Don't leave us out here with these... these bull-men. They look like they want to eat us! Hey wait up!'

The god was all the way up the top of the Olympian stairs to his palace when finally he turned. 'Come on lads; where's your spirit?' he bawled down to them. 'Think top of stairs and join me.'

Both boys immediately thought *top of stairs* and they magically appeared at the top of them, both with jaws dropped at what they were able to do.

18

'That's so cool,' Zac said.

Bray chuckled. 'I'm starting to really like this dream.'

'No dream lads. Wait until we sit for dinner and then we'll talk.' Helios led them into a huge room with the longest table either of them had ever seen. Three chandeliers hung above it and Bray counted twenty-five chairs each side. Wall to wall mirrors ensured you could see every guest from every angle. The table was already set for three.

'How did they know we were coming?' Zac nudged Bray.

A waiter came out. He was human-like but with puppy dog eyes, a hairy face and pointy ears. The waiter had white napkins over his arm and as they sat he placed one of them on each of their laps. 'If you are ready to eat sir?' It spoke to Helios while inclining its head.

Helios nodded. 'Make haste, the boys and I need full stomachs. Serve us now! After that I want privacy in here. We have much to discuss.' Helios turned back to the two boys. 'Hope you both like burger and chips.'

Neither boys could even think about eating but when it came out they wolfed it down.

'That was some burger.' Bray wiped his

plate clean with his fingers and licked them. Zac smiled and nodded in agreement as he did the same. While they ate they took this opportunity to ask questions. At the very least, they knew this single experience was sure to help with their space project. Bray explained what the project was about and Helios showed an unusual interest in this topic. Rather than answer their questions, though, he asked his own questions and even enquired about their teacher.

Bray was just about to mention he'd had enough of being grilled, when the god pushed his plate aside. Both boys watched in silence as he took the napkin from his lap and wiped his mouth. Even if one of them wanted to speak, questions disappeared from their thoughts. Was he using magic on them?

Helios's huge plate was double the size of theirs and yet now, sitting away from him, it looked no bigger than a bread and butter plate. So many strange things didn't add up in Bray's mind.

Helios sat back in his chair, smirking. 'Bet you boys are dying to find out why you are here.'

Bray pushed his plate aside, noticing it didn't shrink the way the god's had. Plucking up courage he leaned forward with his elbows on the table. 'Well I'm guessing it's got something to do with the planets. You haven't stopped firing questions at us since we sat down.' He also sat back in his chair, mimicking the god. 'So you know what we know; it's your turn. Why are we here?'

'You're a smart boy Bray. It's a fine line you tread with that tone though,' Helios warned.

Bray's shoulders sank. He had started to speak that way a lot lately, and he knew his attitude had changed since his new stepdad had moved in with his mum. He reflected for a moment how much he hated his stepdad and wanted it just to be him and his mum again. A light sparked in his mind. If she liked him... could he? He just had to stop feeling so angry all the time. *Maybe give the guy a break.* Bray stared at Helios. Was he talking to him in his mind?

Helios leaned forward and snapped his fingers once. Suddenly above them appeared an image of the planets circling the sun.

'Now watch, my boys; this is your solar system.' He pointed to a bluish planet. 'Here is your planet Earth. It's the third planet from the sun.'

Not to be undermined, Bray rattled of the names of the planets one by one, starting from the sun.' He pointed to each. 'That is Mercury, Venus, Earth, Mars, Jupiter, Saturn, Uranus and Neptune. Pluto isn't part of them anymore.' Bray looked at him smugly.

Adventures of Bray and Zac

'Not bad my boy, but it's not enough to know their names. Take note and see the future.'

As they watched a black jagged rip appeared in the universe. It grew and grew, pushing the sun away from the Earth. This caused the moon to slam into a cluster of stars and it exploded. Next to go was Earth. It was caught up in the explosion and blew into millions of pieces. This set off a chain reaction. The other planets were pushed off course and they began to collide into each other. Some veered towards the sun, causing them to explode on impact. The sky was alight with red and black cinders as the solar system disappeared from sight. As soon as it appeared the vision vanished. All of a sudden the room was in darkness. They heard a clap from where Helios sat and the lights came back on.

Bray's eyes were like saucers. 'Why did you show us that future prediction? It's not prophesied for a billion or so years. We are not doing a project on the end of the universe. And knowing that,' he pointed to the above location where the fire and rocks had floated, 'will not get us an A+. Just frighten the pants off us.' He placed his hands on hips.

Helios's eyebrows were pulled together and matched his frown. 'Listen to me boy, it's not about the project!' He jiggled his finger, the motion making Bray relax back in his chair. *Did he just use calming magic on me?*

'Although,' Helios continued, 'that has taught you a lot about the basics.' He placed two hands clasped together on the table and sat forward. 'It's because you are both gifted. This, coupled with your love of the planets, is why you have both been chosen for this mission.'

Zac pushed his chair back and stood up. 'Mission. You make us sound like we're astronauts or some smart professors. As if two scrawny twelve-year-olds could fix what all you gods together can't.'

'Ah yes, I can see your point. But the gods are not prepared to interfere with this natural disaster. We will live on in a new universe, one of new creations. Therefore the question I put to you is this; if you could, would you do whatever it takes to save your world and this universe?'

Bray pulled Zac back down. 'Let him finish. We have a choice. This won't happen next week right?' Bray guessed this was going to be a long time in the future, if at all in their time. And he was still not convinced this wasn't a dream.

'You have eight days to prevent the split in the universe from forming,' said Helios. 'Once started, it cannot be stopped. The magic to prevent it is found on those very planets you study. Each

Adventures of Bray and Zac

planet has an artefact that you will need. These artefacts were separated and spread over the eight planets many hundreds of years ago. What I have noticed is that they have surfaced, shuffled from deep in the planet crust, almost as if they wait to be retrieved. But it is written that only the effort of innocence that endures this epic challenge will find the key to assemble this weapon.' He gave them a minute to soak in what he had told them so far, before continuing. 'You have to find one each night over eight nights. Once collected, the steroidal magnets will lock them into position and will form an eight-sided suction device. When the top is twisted, it will shoot off in to space. The weapon spins so fast it becomes invisible to the naked eye. With ultrasonic speed its vacuum sucks up the dark energy ready to cause the split, and contains it. The device then vibrates, explodes and lights up the darkness, dissipating all signs of any further dark energy.

'Your mission, boys, is to have all eight pieces ready for take-off at exactly eight minutes past eight on the eighth day of this eighth month to come.' Helios sat back to let what he said sink in and was amused to see the reaction. These two boys were the smartest in the world. They did not know that yet, but both were destined for greatness. On their own death as human saints, they would be rewarded, become immortal and join him amongst the gods.

The Magic Portal

Bray slapped his hands to his cheeks and let out a whistle. 'You're kidding me? We begin now. Here tonight.'

'Not tonight boys! Tomorrow is the first day of the eighth month. For now, I must send you home to get some sleep. When you wake I would advise you two to spend the day wisely. The more you know about each planet the easier your night quest will be. For your homework, the first planet my chariot will take you to is Mercury. Study it well.'

'What! So you're not helping! We do this alone.' Zac looked horrified.

'Well, I can give you the locations but for the rest of it, you're on your own. I am forbidden to help further. The magic will be stronger when coming from the pure bravery of young caring humans.' He sank his head down, a little ashamed that he was unable to assist further.

'But your magic is stronger. You can help. I can see it in your eyes,' Zac challenged him.

'Boys, I will not go against the Heavenly Council. My duty is to the sun. It will take me all my might to save it. For without the sun we will have no light to build a new galaxy once this one is gone.'

Bray nudged Zac. 'Feel like helping me save

Adventures of Bray and Zac

the universe?'

Zac and Bray had dreamed of this type of adventure all their lives; both loved science fiction through and through.

Zac gave a big grin. 'Do you want to help save the universe?'

At the same time each put out a hand and slapped the other's. 'Snap!' they said together.

Staring at one another for a minute, they were so in tune they could read each other like a book. And just as they tackled everything, they would put their hearts and souls into this or die trying. As perfectionists they did not comprehend the word *fail*. They believed they could succeed.

Bray broke from the magic of his best bud, a bond that had him sticking with Zac through thick and thin. His home life might have sucked, but having a best buddy made all his worries go away whenever they were together.

Helios pinched his lips to hide his joy at the courage and fearlessness the boys showed before adding, 'as I said before, you will have to know more than just the names of the planets to survive this challenge that the gods have offered. Knowing the elements and terrain of the planet surfaces are so important if you need to dig or climb. These conditions may delay you from finding each

The Magic Portal

artefact in time. I can use my magic to stop time at eight o'clock at night for eight Earth hours only. The chariot will return to me directly after.' He leaned forward and added seriously, 'whether you are on it or not.'

'But we don't know how to climb mountains, if that's what you mean,' said Zac.

'And where will we get the gear to complete these challenges?' asked Bray.

'All you need will be provided. And like now, just as long as the chariot is within a direct eight NAVks radius, which is eighty Earth kilometres, it will allow you to breathe oxygen. But I warn, if you go deep inside a crater or walk around a mountain you could lose its protective power.

'I'm almost certain the chariot will prevent you suffering frost bite and the cold as you move farther out into the solar system. After all it did prevent you getting scorched by the sun. But to be sure, you must suit up before each expedition as the chariot alone may not be enough to protect your frail human bodies. I have never had to test out the magic of my ride on boys before.'

'Great.' Bray's shoulders dropped. 'And where do we find space costumes that fit. We aren't as big as any astronauts I've ever heard of.'

'That's true. Therefore I will also supply you

with the necessary protective gear. As for your last question, you're smart lads. I'm sure you can use that electronic device I see you using.'

'Hey what!' Zac squinted. 'Our phones?'

'He's talking about google.' Bray shook his head at Helios. 'It's called a laptop! You gods don't get around much, do you?'

'Hope your abilities match your arrogance my boy.' Helios eyed Bray.

With that comment, the room began to spin and they were back in the cloud as before. Sparks of magic snapped and crackled and within minutes they were in Zac's room.

Chapter Three

Mission Eight

The sound of Bray's stepdad's voice startled him. 'Bray, you're going to be late. Up now! I told your mother I'd drop you off at school on my way to work.' He pulled the blanket off him. 'Good you're dressed already. What happened… you get up and then lie down for another snooze? This is your third and final call. Next time it's with cold water.'

'Okay! Geez keep your shirt on.' Bray struggled off the bed and snatched up his two-way. 'You up, Zac?' he said as he turned to pick up his backpack off the floor.

Busily he piled stuff in it off his desk while his stepdad watched. 'Shoes!' he growled.

Bray sat and slid on his runners when Zac's voice came through the speaker. 'I slept in. Meet you outside.'

Adventures of Bray and Zac

Bray clicked on the talk button. 'Eishol's taking us to school. Come over, he's in a rush or something. Talk about a control freak.' He sneered at his stepdad as he pushed past him out the door, ducking as a hand came out to clip him one for being cheeky.

'Lucky boy!' Eishol snapped as he followed him out. 'You have one smart mouth on you young man.'

Bray ignored him. Instead he detoured into the kitchen, and snatched up the brown paper bag from the bench. His mum still dutifully made his lunch each day, only today there were two bags.

'Take them both. Looks like your mate won't have time to get breakfast either,' Eishol said. 'He can have mine and I'll grab something from the cafe next to work.' He stuffed the second paper bag into Bray's backpack before he could say no.

'But hang on a minute... she never makes you lunch,' Bray said. 'You knew she made them for me and Zac. How did Mum know Zac would sleep in too? How'd she know I'd be sharing my sandwich today?'

'What, you think your mum's psychic? You think too much lad. Now get moving. I have somewhere more important to be. Look, your mate's already at the car.'

The Magic Portal

When they pulled up at school, Bray couldn't get out the car quick enough. He tugged Zac out and didn't turn to say goodbye. He was still cross at his stepdad who was so... so, annoying.

'Study up well boys. No time to muck about,' his stepdad called out.

Bray took big strides to avoid having to interact with him any further.

'That was weird.' Zac came up beside him. 'Why did Eishol, I mean your stepdad, say that?'

'Why anything?' Bray adjusted the heavy bag on his shoulders. 'Eishol never spoke all the way here and when he does, crap comes out. That's what I'm living with now. He speaks like he's in another era, and so bossy all the time. Oh, except when Mum's around.' Bray rolled his eyes. 'Then he acts like father of the year.'

'Shush, we're here and we have moody Miss Starr lurking. She hates us talking in the hall,' Zac whispered. His hand reached for the class door knob but the door opened before he touched it.

'Get inside you two. You're late!' Miss Starr had heard them after all.

Zac went to apologise but she put her hand up to silence him. 'No excuses. Get to your desks and open your science text book to page forty-five.

We are studying Mercury today. Lucky for you both there was a fire drill and we have only now returned. And please refrain from talking in the hallway when class has begun. I don't care what reason you think you have,' she chastised them.

Lunch time couldn't have come quickly enough for Bray. They had crammed in so much reading! Add this to Miss Starr's teachings and the pair of them were ready to bust with the excitement from what they had learned. Out in the corridor they high fived each other and ran out to their favourite spot under a largely overgrown gum tree where they went to eat lunch each day. The branches hung so low they were almost hidden from all those haters of geeks; the ones that flaunted in the sunshine and lounged around on tables... their body language saying, *look at me!*

This was the geeks' hideout where they could stay mostly unnoticed, safe from playground bullies. Very rarely did they get bothered; most of the time they were forgotten. Out of sight out of mind was their key to surviving.

'This will do.' Bray flung his backpack on the soft ground, pulled out a lunch bag and handed it to Zac. 'Here, Mum made an extra.'

'She must have ESP. No way did I get time to slap a sandwich together this morning. And you know my mum's not cool like yours.' He ripped open the bag and stuffed nearly half the sandwich in his mouth. 'Yum I love your mum's food.' He chuckled and spat crumbs as he talked, making them both laugh.

Bray chewed half his sandwich as he went over his notes from class. Zac finished his and, still hungry, snatched up Bray's other half and took a big bite of it.

'You can have it.' Bray grinned. 'It is so not fair. The way you eat you should be my weight yet you're a bean pole. I swear you have a hollow body.'

'Sure you don't mind.' Zac had already shoved the other quarter in his mouth.

'Bit late now.' Bray chuckled and lay back on the grass. 'Seriously I'm not that hungry. I'm too excited. Just want it to be eight o'clock so we can go visit this planet. Zac, aren't you just busting?' He held the picture of Mercury above him, and used it to shade the light that found its way through some of the leaves.

'Course I am. That's why I couldn't stop eating. I want to eat my way through time so it's night time now. Geez what would happen if the school knew? Two nerds were chosen out of the billions of strong athletic type people around the globe.' Zac shook his head. 'They could have picked anyone. But they chose us.' His eyes were bright, happy and alert.

Bray rolled onto his side, leaning on a bent arm. 'Yes why us?'

Zac shot him one of his wide toothy grins. 'Because they wanted the best.'

Chapter Four

Mecury

'Zac hurry, it's almost 8 o'clock,' Bray called out. He was sitting cross-legged on the floor with the book that acted as a portal in front of him.

Zac skidded into the circle they created as the book began to smoke. 'I forgot to lock the door. Don't want the folks finding me gone. I set up a recording if they knock and had to switch it on too. Good to go now.'

'I did the same!' Bray whispered. 'But try harder Zac. You have to be more organized or I will be shooting off without you.'

Zac was about to say he hadn't thought of that when they started to lift off the ground and spin before being sucked into the book. As before they made a grab for each other and didn't stop screaming until, *"thump!"* They landed.

'Hi, I am Ochimus, son of Helios. My father has much on his plate of late. It is I who will greet you in the failing light.'

'He sure looks like Helios.' Bray eyed the speaker from behind.

'Even the same build,' Zac agreed.

They were once again on the chariot flying across the sky with a sun almost disappearing before their eyes. A moon became visible as the horses landed on ground and the chariot came to a skidding halt. Both boys held on for grim death.

Ochimus let out a whistle. 'Wahoo!' he called out with his fist in the air. 'What a ride.' He jumped off the chariot. 'All yours boys.' He handed Bray the reins when he stood.

'What! We don't even know how to drive this thing,' Zac said.

'The horses know where to take you. Just hold the reins and give them a good hard flick to get the horses moving and pull on them when you want to stop. You're not dragging the sun so your journey is simple.' He snapped his fingers and a sack appeared in the back with them. 'It's magical, boys. All you discussed today is there, plus a couple of extra items of my father's choice. Oh and watch the time. You have eight hours from now.' Two watches appeared on their wrists. The eight hours had already started counting down. 'Now you're both synchronized with me. If you're not back on the chariot in eight hours, it leaves without you. The magic will have it transported back here.'

'But without the magic of the chariot, how do we survive?' Bray said.

'Not my problem.' Ochimus turned and walked away, whistling and with a spring in his step.

'Stuff them Zac, let's get this done. We don't need any of them.' Bray held the reins, gave them one good hard shake and *crack*! This made the horses jolt forward, putting both boys on their backsides. They laughed out loud.

'Better be a bit gentler.' Bray got to his feet, helped Zac up and recovered the reins.

'Give me a go.' Zac tried to snatch them.

'You can drive on the way home.' Bray felt proud of his first duty. 'Zac, this is a blast.' He grinned with pride. 'You and me, bud. Aren't we the luckiest kids ever?'

'Surely are!' Zac pointed to a planet looming ahead. 'How do we get from A to B so fast? I think that's Mercury coming up. It looks like brown marble.'

'With craters,' Bray agreed. 'Geez, I forgot. Take the reins Zac. I have to get that device thing out of my pocket and set us as close to the artefact as I can.' He turned it on. 'This thing has a name. *NAVscan* just flashed up. It's the first time I've had to turn it on.'

'Good, you can stop calling it a device or a thingy.' Zac put his hand out for the NAVscan. 'Give me a go of it.'

'If you hand the reins over to use this you know you won't get them back.' Bray was serious. He was full of pride being able to drive the chariot of Helios.

'Forget it then. If it's a choice between driving the horses across the sky or playing with a gadget, sorry, but there's no competition. Happy to do this and you can do the directing.' Zac turned and flicked the reins.

'You're kidding. This thing, I mean this NAVscan...' He corrected himself before Zac did. 'It's the coolest navigation tool I've used. You know, it only took me one maths class to work it out, and that was only the basics. I reckon it does so much more.' Bray looked back at the device. 'That was quick, we're here.'

'Wow that was fast. These horses sure can fly.' Zac grinned at his explorer friend.

The Magic Portal

Bray shuddered with the thrill of being able to walk on another planet. 'It's there Zac. Pull on the left rein to move the horses closer. We need to be on the far side of the Rachmaninoff crater.'

'Easy peasy.' Zac soon had the horses diverting slightly. It was enough to put them on target. 'See they don't know everything.' He beamed for being able to handle the majestic fire-darting steeds.

'Get ready to slow them, *now*!' Bray put his hand up and then dropped it.

Zac gently pulled the horses up, missed the mark and circled them until they were in the exact spot. The chariot and horses hovered fifty metres off the ground. The ledge they had to land on was only five metres from the left side of them. The horses couldn't get any closer due to the jagged way it jutted out.

'You're good at this Zac. How about you drive from now on and I'll navigate.'

'Really? Wow, that gives me a big head,' Zac said.

'You deserve it. Good job.' Bray slapped at Zac's hand he held up.

'Well, we got this far.' Zac's mood was on a high. He turned to Bray. 'What now nature boy?'

Adventures of Bray and Zac

Bray dug around in the bag that had been stored on the chariot. He pulled out two ropes that were already knotted. Not only that, but they were attached to a plank of wood making a platform they could stand on.

'Zac! Don't think we have to climb. This must have a pulley system.' He tried to get the ropes to come out with the bag but the sack was fully lodged into the floor of the cart and wouldn't budge.

Bray tossed the plank and rope over the side of the cart. It didn't disappear over the edge so he guessed it was magical and would lower once they were on it.

'What else is there?' Zac tried to peek over Bray's head.

'This.' Bray's hand appeared holding a hand-held pick. 'Remember we were going to ask for something to dig around the box in case it is in the rocks?'

The next to come out were two protective jump suits complete with attached gloves, boots and full facemask hoodies. The material was thin and transparent.

'Well if they are in our bag, we must have to wear them.' Bray started to place one light-weight, clear material suit over his clothes.

'It's freezing.' Zac yanked his on fast. 'Good thing they stretch over everything. And check out the balaclava. Even has clear eye patches so I can see and the material on the mouth allows me to breathe. If you can hear me, then we can also talk to each other.'

'Yep, I can hear you fine. Helios has thought of everything.'

Once the protective gear was on and then magically zipped up, leaving no tell-tale signs of the join, they both agreed it felt much warmer. They were glad Helios had looked after them as ice had started to form, covering the surface of the planet in a white blanket.

'What's this?' Bray removed the last item in the bag.

Zac felt it and it vibrated. 'It's blue and moves.' He jumped back as the bulging eyes on tentacles looked directly at him.

In their minds the thing spoke. 'I am your guide. They call us Ercs. We are red when annoyed, blue when happy. We belong to the Mercs tribe and have protected the artefact you seek for thousands of years.'

'You protect it from whom?' Bray's eyes were wide.

'Witch Rhapsody,' said the Erc.

Both the boys' jaws dropped at hearing a witch was involved.

'Yes, the witch works for the gods who oppose you finding these artifacts. I am here to help,' said the Erc.

'A witch... here!' Zac turned to his friend, uncertain.

'Zac, settle! I doubt Helios would drop us off on an alien planet without help to survive. Little Erc here must be a guide from our friend the god because there's a witch here. '

'Guess so but...' Zac rubbed his nose. 'But what if Erc can't protect us and she kidnaps us? What if we can't get back to the chariot in time? I mean, I thought these planets were uninhabitable.'

'Well we know the gods live on these planets because we have seen Helios and his palace. So it's possible an immortal witch may live here. As for the *what ifs*... let's worry about them when and if they ever happen. Remember Zac, this is our dream and a witch in the mix is nothing we haven't imagined before.'

'It's coming true isn't it? All that stuff we wrote stories about, alien invasions, going into space and what we would find...' said Zac.

'Exactly, and if this was one of our stories, we'd want to be right here, living it. Am I right?' Bray smiled. 'So let's get on with this and enjoy the ride.' He punched Zac's arm to snap him out of it. He knew Zac wished this to be a really scary cool adventure too, but fear gripped him. Still no response, but Bray knew how to bring him around. 'Hey… you can stay here if you want. You can protect the cart. I'll take Erc with me and be back in a jiff.'

'Bull-crap. I'm not staying here alone with some crazy witch flying around on a broomstick. No way. I'm coming.' Zac picked up the Erc and, noticing a pocket in his suit, pulled it out and put the furry Erc inside. Once it got comfy, its tentacle-eyeballs stuck out the top of the pocket.

He thought it best to carry the critter, believing something so small would slow them down if it was to move along beside them. Zac gave his furry little body a tickle. 'You right there fella?'

In the meantime, Bray was in his element. He had won the battle against Zac's nerves and they were off on the first of many adventures. He slipped on his backpack and moved fast so he could help Zac over the side of the chariot and onto the plank before he lost confidence again.

'Hold on tight,' Bray warned as he stepped over the side and onto it too. Once his feet hit the plank it started to move in a jerky motion towards the surface. 'You have to admit, this is better than climbing down a rope.' He kept talking and tried to calm Zac down. His friend's breathing was so heavy Bray thought he may need to tip one of the sandwiches out of its wrap and pass him the paper bag to hyperventilate into. But as soon as they reached the ledge, Zac took a deep breath and calmed down on his own.

'You okay now?'

Zac furrowed his eyebrows together. 'Of course I am. Geez can't a guy have a phobia?'

Bray was surprised at his sudden defensive reply. He was not used to his friend speaking to him like that, and it was on the tip of his tongue to call him a skirt.

Zac stopped and grabbed him by the shirt, pulling him close. 'I dare you to.'

'What!' Bray gulped then gave a nervous chuckle. 'I didn't say a thing.' He scoffed. 'Is that thing we brought reading my mind, it is, isn't it? Dobber Erc.'

Zac chuckled and let him go. 'You got my secret; how did you guess?'

'The traitor, tell the little freak it's toast if it can't zip it.'

'Erc said he was just checking how smart you were. He needs you thinking on your feet if the witch comes snooping around.'

'When did he start communicating telepathically? I can't hear him,' said Bray.

'Once we were on firm ground he began to communicate. He tells me he can direct it at whoever he wants,' Zac relayed.

'Why not talk to me?' Bray asked.

Zac was silent. Then he relayed the answer, amused. 'He said he doesn't like you because you talk and think too much. He has asked if you'd shut up and keep quiet so he can concentrate and direct us.'

'Little furry nit. I'll give him shut up and be quiet. When you put the runt down, I may just squash him with my big fat noisy boot. Keep him quiet too,' Bray mumbled.

As he trudged after them, he decided to stay quiet but only because he had a hard time keeping up. It had also become harder to breathe the further from the chariot they moved. Yet Zac tackle the rugged terrain, crawled over huge boulders and down deep crevices with energy to burn. It was then Bray understood. The little Erc was giving him the power to handle the terrain and atmosphere.

'Hey Zac, wait up. It's not you. And you don't have special powers. Our Erc guide is helping you.'

Zac stopped and turned, surprised to see Bray puffing and needing to stop for a rest. He normally had more stamina when they went out on hikes with the school.

Bray sat on a rock and pulled out the NAVscan. He was sure they should have reached the artefact long before now.

Zac came back to sit with him, worried that Bray didn't look so good. 'Sorry. I'm glad you stopped for a break, I'm exhausted too. Are you okay?' Zac pulled the furry alien out of his pocket and put it on the ground while he rested. The second he did so, the spell was broken. He looked around; no chariot in sight. 'Where are we?' He realised they were deep inside the wall of the crater.

'You tell me Zac. I've been following you and that thing,' Bray huffed, annoyed. He finally thought to look at the NAVscan. 'This is saying we're a couple of miles north of the artefact.'

Zac settled beside him. 'I think we're in trouble Bray.'

Bray agreed. 'That alien has taken us to an area where the rocks are shielding us from the magic of the chariot. We must head back immediately. I can hardly breathe.'

'The little runt tried to kill us.' Zac only just felt the restriction of air now he was disconnected from the Erc. 'Where is the lying life-sucker.' They looked around for the Erc but it was gone. 'Come on Bray, let me help you up.' He stood and put a hand out.

Bray gratefully took it. 'Thanks buddy. You're right, if we don't get back to the chariot soon, we'll die out here. Now the Erc has gone, I'm finding it even harder to breathe. He must have used a special power to surround us with oxygen. What he didn't count on is us not only having the use of a god's chariot but me living with the weirdest stepdad ever.'

He pulled off his backpack, unzipped it and pulled out two things that looked like compact gas masks; something you would see the Special Forces use. Both were unusually light and had a miniature 02 cylinder attached. 'Here put this on.' He handed one to Zac. 'It will help you breathe.'

'What do you mean, weirdest ever stepdad? Are these from him?' Zac put it on.

'Must be. Well let's put it this way, no way would my mum have put them in my bag. And Eishol was the only other person who had access to it. It was him who handed it to me when I left the house. I figure he can either see into the future and saw we needed them or he is just one big weirdo. I lean towards weirdo,' Bray said.

'Me too.' Zac nodded in agreement. 'Helios said no human will ever learn about our mission and he would know. That dude can see into the future.'

'Well however they ended up in my bag, it was only pure luck I noticed them. I stuffed a couple of things in my backpack that we didn't need from the stash Helios left us. That's when I noticed the masks. It couldn't have been anyone else,' Bray said. He put his apparatus on and secured it behind his ears. 'I forgot all about them when the Erc turned up. I think he made me forget because I only remembered now he's gone.'

They stopped for a rest.

'Glad you did.' Zac's lungs didn't feel as restricted now and he was able to say what he guessed Bray would be also thinking. 'Do you reckon we'll make it back before that evil Erc stowaway gets where he's going? My guess is he was protecting the artefact from us.'

'Have to agree. Bet he is working for Witch Rhapsody,' Bray said. 'Though we've only the Erc's word for it she even exists.'

Zac stood up. 'Then let's get a move on. The

The Magic Portal

Erc's only small. If you're feeling better, we could run and try to beat him.'

'Much better now.' Bray jumped to his feet. 'I've worked out where we are, too.' He popped the NAVscan in his pocket and began to jog.

Zac passed him, laughing. 'Slow coach,' he said.

'Is that right?' Bray picked up speed. 'Was only going slow so you could keep up.' He passed Zac.

Both raced, breathing heavily into their masks and stumbling over rocks. Racing gave them the spark they needed to get back to the artefact quickly.

Finally at the destination, which was very close to the ledge where they'd met the Erc, they hid behind a rock, debating. 'The Erc is there with a really old lady. Bet she is the witch. He beat us,' Zac whispered. 'Horrid creature. He got us lost and tried to suffocate us, but he didn't count on you, Bray. You kept the air masks a secret. If you had even thought about them when he was near us, he would have picked it up in his thoughts. Maybe he'd have dissolved them with magic or something more sinister.'

Bray's eyes widened. 'Like set my backpack on fire or loosen the straps so it fell down the cliff and deep into the crater.'

'Or that. Glad you didn't leave your weirdness at home.' Zac grinned.

Bray smiled and kept his voice low. 'Well he must have switched off or he'd know we're here.'

'Played us for fools,' Zac said.

'I know, and to think we believed the liar. I agree with you, she has to be Witch Rhapsody. And as for Erc, there is no way I believe he belongs to some Mercs tribe (whatever that is). He helps the witch, look at them you can tell they are friends.'

They saw Erc point to the chariot and with a cackling laugh, the old lady lifted her skirt and dashed off towards it. Her laugh alone confirmed what she really was.

'What do we do now?' Zac panicked as they watched the witch run to the chariot.

'Erc's going too. Let's just go do what we we're meant to do and get the artefact while they're gone. If the witch is able to work the pulley and get up into the chariot, it will surely not leave without us on board. One job at a time,' Bray whispered.

'You're right. Let's do what we came here to do, get us our piece of the missile or whatever the thing is called. Look, the box is over there?'

'Yes I can see it,' Bray said. 'Why didn't we see it before?'

'Because the Erc distracted us, of course.'

Both boys crept over to the box and started removing the rocks, but couldn't budge it from the ground.

'What do we do now?' Zac sat on the rock next to it and leant on the box. The engraving on the lid lit up and he moved quickly away. 'I didn't do anything.' He looked at Bray, worried.

Suddenly it shook and moved outwards from where it was lodged. There was a noise like cogs turning and a drawer slid out. Inside was a blue and pink eight-sided object.

'Gee Zac, this alien technology is amazing,' said Bray. 'How does an object that resembles a CD, only with eight sides, turn into a weapon?'

Zac shrugged. 'Got me beat. But we've both watched *Transformers* enough times to know it's possible.'

Bray snatched up the disc that was heavier than expected and to keep it safe, slipped it inside his pocket with the NAVscan. As he did so the lid slammed down and the artefact box moved back into the ground where it had been lodged before. Both boys jumped to their feet and ran as fast as

Adventures of Bray and Zac

their legs would allow them, towards the chariot.

Bray's arm shot out and grabbed hold of Zac's arm, pulling him along. Both suddenly had superhuman speed and before long they had passed the witch and Erc. Balanced together on the plank, they puffed loudly as they tried to catch their breath.

'Thank goodness for magic.' Bray started laughing.

'The alien disc sure wanted to be with us, hey Bray. It was the disc - wasn't it?'

Bray grinned. 'It had us almost flying, didn't it.'

Zac nodded. 'Glad you grabbed hold of me when you felt yourself speed up, or I might still be back there.'

When they were safe and sound inside the chariot, Bray slapped an arm around him. 'Zac, I would never leave you behind.' Bray was serious. 'Never!'

'Thanks pal, I feel the same.' Zac put his arm around him and ruffled the top of his head with his knuckles. 'Now let's get out of here, hero. Want me to take the reins?'

'Gladly. I want to check this disc out. Make

sure it's not broken from being tossed around in my pocket.' Bray heard Zac call out the horses' names; 'Wake up, Pyrios, Aeos, Aethon and Phlegon! Job is done. Take us home...' Bray heard the *crack* which sounded out when the reins were given a good flick and the horses leapt forward. They were in the air for only seconds before the cloud substance appeared and they were being tossed onto the floor in Zac's bedroom.

'What happened?' Bray checked his watch. 'It's 4am.' He turned to Zac. 'We've been gone eight hours.'

'This means Erc is a no-good stowaway who had us walking for hours under some kind of spell.' Zac was wide eyed, his mouth still open in a surprised manner.

'We've learned one valuable lesson tonight Zac. We don't trust the natives.'

'You can say that again.'

'We have learned one valuable lesson tonight Zac. We don't trust the natives.' Bray started laughing at his joke.

'Ha, ha funny.' Zac frowned. 'I wonder why the witch didn't take the artefact? Why did she and the Erc go for the chariot?'

'I guess they wanted to strand us there and

kill us,' said Bray. It was a nasty thought.

Zac shook himself. 'Well, we're still alive, so bad luck to them. Let's check we didn't snap the artefact in half on landing.' He moved over to help Bray up.

Once on his feet Bray shook off his backpack and found the disc still where he had shoved it. 'All good. Nothing broken. Do you want me to hide this at my place?' He held the eight sided disc up. 'After tonight, learning about alien lifeforms that can stow away, even in the god's magic bag, we better be careful.' Bray looked worried.

'Good idea! Bet they can find their way here into my room... through the book.' Zac picked up the book. 'I'm hiding it in the bottom of my filing cabinet just in case. If anyone does come through it they will find themselves in a locked drawer.' He chuckled. 'Wow, that was some adventure.' He sat on his desk chair after locking the book away.

Now feeling more relaxed Bray chuckled too. 'Can you believe what happened? We have survived our first mission. First piece of... recover the Black Hole deflector... tick!' He made a tick sign in the air with his finger, laughed and got up, doing a silly happy dance.

Zac joined him, going... 'ah ha ah ha!'

They collapsed back on the bed exhausted.

Sleep took them both. Bray's last thought was he'd better be getting home or his stepdad would be furious in the morning when he wasn't in his own bed.

Thump! Thump! Thump!

'Bray, are you in there! Wake up boys! Bray, Zac, open up.'

Zac got up and unlocked the door. Bray's stepdad stood with his hands on his hips. 'I was worried sick, boy.'

Bray had rolled on the floor during the night and stretched out on the fluffy mat. Rubbing his eyes he sat up. 'We studied until late. Is Mum mad?'

'I didn't tell her. Instead, I offered to take you to school.' He lifted up two bags of sandwiches. 'She left these. I said you were hungry so she made two again.'

'Why stick up for me?' Bray got up and picked up his backpack. He felt for the disc. It was there but with his stepdad watching on, how could he hide it? Was he game enough to stash it in his locker at school? They were broken into all the time.

'No concern of yours; why. But if you want me to keep covering for you, it's time you let me in on your little secret. Just what are you two boys up to? This is night two you've woken looking panic-stricken and barely alert because you've slept so little.'

Zac finished putting on his shoes and socks, and, walking past Bray's stepdad, took both prepared lunches and unzipped his own backpack. He put them inside. Artfully he navigated his way past Eishol and slipped out the door. 'I'll wait in the car.' He disliked confrontation and figured it was best left to Bray.

'Well son? I'm waiting for an explanation.'

'Eishol, not now. Can you just trust me we are not doing anything illegal? It's something really important though.'

He stood looking at Bray for a few seconds, studying him. 'You know if you have something important in your bag I wouldn't be taking it to school.'

'What makes you think I have something?'

'It's the way you're clutching it and those sweat beads on your brow are a certain give-away.'

Bray sat down on Zac's bed. 'I can't tell you what this is about. For a start you would never believe me.'

'Try trusting me, I might surprise you?'

Bray shook his head. 'I don't even know

The Magic Portal

you. I sure as hell don't trust you. But you're right about one thing; I do have to run to my room and stash something.'

'Then run, boy! It's almost time for the bell to ring.'

Bray looked up with a slight grin. It was the first time he had smiled at Eishol ever. 'You trust me?' he said.

'Go before I change my mind.'

Bray let out an excited whistle and ran past him, down the stairs and across the road, not stopping the pace until he was through the front door and to his room. Fleetingly he reflected on why the front door had been left open but with no time to think further, he looked around for a good hiding spot. With a quick scan of the room he spotted the broken CD player that should have gone out in the last kerb-side collection. The opening was large. He took the disc from his pocket and pressed it into the slot. 'Perfect fit!' He punched the air with his fist. Carefully he placed it back on the shelf right on top of the dust mark. It looked as if it had never been moved.

Pleased the artefact was in a safe place he ran back through the house and clicked the lock, before slamming the door shut and locking it behind him. In the car he was still fiddling with the seatbelt when the car sped off. His stepdad was obviously anxious to be somewhere else. Bray didn't know what he did for work but it must have been important. *Why always in such a rush?* Bray didn't believe for one second it was to get them to school to keep them out of trouble. *And how come the sudden interest, caring we eat, letting me off with not saying what we were doing to make us sleep in and lastly, making sure we got to school on time?* None of this added up. He was sure Eishol was only being nice for his mum's sake. Yet up in the room there was something between them. He eyed Eishol, who as usual drove in silence, and decided lack of sleep must heighten the imagination.

At school Bray followed Zac in quietly to the classroom.

When they entered Miss Starr yelled at them for being late, yet again. 'Catch up boys! Pages 50 to 55. Read, then answer the questions from the blackboard in your notebooks.'

All other thoughts left Bray when he saw what they would study today. Back in the adventure, both boys glanced at each other with the biggest grin. They were studying Venus; the planet next to Mercury. Their next quest.

Excited, they started reading.

Venus is similar size to Earth's density,

composition and gravity. Atmosphere is 90 times heavier than Earth's. It consists mainly of carbon dioxide, clouds of sulphuric acid and traces of water. This dense atmosphere holds in the heat. It keeps the planet in a prolonged molten state. It makes Venus the hottest world in the solar system. The temperatures reach 465 degrees Celsius, hot enough to melt lead. Most of the surface is covered by flat, smooth plains marred by thousands of volcanoes, some of which are still active. The rest of the surface is mountainous ranges.

After reading, Bray realised this was going to be one very hot home world to visit. He wrote on a piece of paper. *I hope the artefact is stashed in the mountains and not in a volcano.* He handed it to Zac who read it and nodded in agreement.

Chapter Five

Bully Grogan

The bell rang for lunch. Bray and Zac ran to their spot under the tree. The thrill of being the chosen ones to go and experience Venus first hand was hard to contain. They high fived each other and let out a yahoo before sitting under their favourite tree.

'It's got no moon. It's going to be pitch black.' Zac flopped on the grass. He immediately thought of food. He pulled his backpack off and dug around for the brown-paper lunch bags Eishol had given him that morning.

'I'm so excited I have to eat.' He handed the paper bag he felt was the lightest to Bray. 'Here's yours. Remind me to tell your mum that she is the best lunch maker ever.' He took his first bite and a quarter disappeared into his mouth. 'Oh this is heaven in a slab.' He wiped his mouth with the back of his hand. Satisfied he was eating he noticed Bray sat quietly. He had been as excited as he was only seconds ago. He watched him slowly, mechanically take out the first half of his sandwich, clearly deep in thought.

'You okay?' Zac asked.

Bray nodded. 'It's what you said about it being dark on Venus. I find it strange that I happen to have two hats with lights on them and two small but powerful torches in my survival kit that Eishol packed for me. I saw them last night when I dug around to find those breathing masks for us. I'm most likely overthinking it. But who is my stepdad? I mean, I know nothing about him.'

Zac started laughing. 'You're right, you're over thinking. Let's face it; lighting is the first thing we would think of to pack as well. I mean, he would have been concerned about power failure, that's all.'

Bray bit into the half sandwich he held. It was freshly cooked chicken with a moreish flavour he hadn't tasted before. 'You're right, twice. He is just a stepdad and no one special, and my mum has outdone herself with lunch.' He scoffed it down and picked up the other half before Zac could snatch it up.

Zac grinned. 'Told you it was good.' He screwed up his bag into a little ball and tossed it into the bin near them. 'Yes!' He cheered as it went in.

'First time for everything.' Bray did the same and blinked with surprise as his went in too.

'Shot!' Zac high fived him.

'What did Mum put in those sangas?' Bray grinned.

They both shrugged. Too many things were going on to give too much thought to the idea that sports-wise they may have just been late bloomers.

Lying on their stomachs, Zac pulled out his satellite notepad and Bray opened up to Venus in his workbook. Both intended to study.

'Hi boys... getting cosy are we?' The school bully and his mates had found them.

'Get lost, we're studying,' Bray snapped at them and when he turned to see who it was, he could have eaten his tongue for the attitude he gave.

'Think they need a lesson again.' Grogan, the nastiest one, who hadn't spoken before, grabbed both bags and shook all the contents on the ground. 'What have we here?' Grogan held the safety kit in his large fat fingers. The guy was a monster, not at all normal. His size prevented him sitting in the normal chairs. He had to drag two together, one for each cheek, when attending class. Everyone hated him but they were also scared of him.

Bray sucked back. 'Sorry man, thought you were someone else. I swear I didn't mean to be rude and I take it back. Please don't wreck our stuff. We will do anything.'

'Too late... this is mine. He shoved the safety pack at the smallest member of his gang to hold. Come on boys, let's show these rich brats not to stuff with us.'

After the bullies left, a teacher came to their rescue. Both stood in their underpants. Their shorts and shirts were up in the tree.

The maths teacher was tall and fit. He stretched up, easily retrieving their clothes. Not getting out of them the bullies' names he frowned and instead of disciplining them further, gave them the hurry up to get to class. The bell had rung. The ogling gang that cheered the bullies on had fully dispersed into class and watched out windows. Bray was glad the overgrown branches prevented them seeing his embarrassment of yet again getting them both into this predicament.

'Sorry Zac.' Bray was flushed red in the face.

Zac turned to him, pulling leaves out of his undies and putting his shorts back on. 'Last time it was my fault. Don't worry. When we save this world they will fall at our feet and ask for forgiveness.'

'Like that's ever going to happen. We can't tell anyone so how will anyone even know it was us?' Bray grumbled unhappily while bending down and picked up the contents of his bag strewn all over the ground. He was glad he hadn't bought the artefact. 'And what are we going to do without the safety kit? The lights in the hats would have been perfect.'

Zac scrambled on hands and knees grabbing his items. 'My satellite notepad's gone. They flogged my tablet. It's got all our stuff on it we've been doing.' Zac's throat closed. He could hardly breathe... he was panic-stricken.

'Looking for this?' Grogan stood leaning against the trunk of the tree. In one hand he held Zac's notepad and in the other Bray's safety kit. The teacher had gone in after telling them to get a move on to class. To find themselves alone with the biggest bully in the school had them shaking in their boots.

'W...what are you going to do?' Zac shook.

'Well it looks to me like you boys could use a partner. I want in. I want to come with you to Venus tonight.'

Bray turned to Zac. 'What did you do? Have you recorded everything?'

Zac nodded. 'I never dreamed anyone would get into it. I have a triple password.'

'And you thought I was just an idiot bully with no brains. Why do you think I pick on you? Not once have you ever invited me to join you to share in an intellectual conversation. About time you stopped hiding and looked around. What you guys are doing here is... *Frigging Awesome!* and there's not one kid here that wouldn't help if they knew.' He slapped his leg. 'I repeat, *Frigging Awesome*, you guys.'

Bray couldn't help smiling. 'Yep we think so too. But this is top secret Grogan. Not even our parents know. As for bringing you in on it, only we two can go. The chariot wouldn't fit you in the back when we land. There's only enough room for us. But hey, we are really struggling studying up each day for the next mission. So maybe you could come over after school and help.'

'Help with what?' Grogan didn't look happy about not going.

'Well we have to first get the location, look it up and once we know what surrounds the artefact, we have to work out a way to get to it. The last one was in a crater so we used ropes.'

Grogan had a strange twinkle in his eye and his mouth twisted in a grin. 'As I thought,

The Magic Portal

you two have just concocted this story to try and make friends. Well it won't work. You were too forthcoming and accepted me far too easily into your confidence. But since I enjoyed the story I'll leave you to it this time. But as you write this bullshit fantasy I want to read it. Expect me here tomorrow for the next chapter. But it better be good or else. Or you know what will happen.' He tossed their belongings to them, and strode off.

Both boys caught their possessions in midair. For once, luck was on their side. Faded were the memories of embarrassment as they entered their next class. They were just happy they had escaped a second encounter with Grogan. A story was all he wanted and from now on if they did as he said, they would be okay.

Chapter Six

Later that night after dinner, both boys huddled around the computer screen. Using the NAVscan, Bray found the coordinates of the next artefact. 'It's in the mountain ranges.'

They both sighed with relief, grateful it wasn't buried deep in hot volcanic lava.

'There.' Zac froze the frame. 'Is that it?'

Bray looked at the NAVscan again. 'It only shows that it is somewhere in the Maxwell Mountain Range. Gee whiz, the coordinates are not so vague. The heat up there must be playing havoc with the NAVscan.' He rubbed his head. 'So if Maxwell Range is giving us a reading of 870 km long and the mountains reach up to some 11.3 km high... that gives me an idea. Zac, find the highest mountain.'

'No probs.' Zac was already on it and moved the alien satellite to show the highest peak in the Maxwell Ranges.

The screen paused. 'Here's the highest mountain.' Zac pointed.

As the satellite moved it gave them a visual of each side of the mountain. It was ten minutes to go before the portal opened and they had still not found it. Just about ready to give up and check out another mountain, Bray spotted a triangle sticking out of the dirt. It was approximately 300 metres up from the base of the mountain. 'That has to be it!' he yelled, excited.

Zac got as close as they could and the piece of box sticking out did have a marking on it similar to the last. 'Phew. Thank goodness we found it. I was starting to panic we would be going up there with no idea where it was. So brainiac, how do we get to it? The horses won't get the chariot close enough for us to dangle out and grab it. The mountain looks awfully steep and those shards of rocks are most likely razor sharp. Looks slippery too; not an easy climb.'

'But there is no other way Zac. We are going to have to climb.' Bray held the book. 'Hope this works.' He grinned at Zac. 'We need climbing gear,' he said to the book hoping Helios was listening.

Zac looked up rock climbing gear and added. 'Traditional rock climbing gear.' He eyed Bray. 'That's the equipment we learned to use at Boy Tuff Camp last summer, right?'

The book snapped open and the room filled with white mist. The portal had opened. It was time. They grabbed for their backpacks and as they swung them over their shoulders, the room spun. Freaked out initially as this part of the trip generally made them feel like throwing up due to its fast, twisty, intense swirl, they grabbed for each other, but missed. They were snatched from Zac's room and taken into the portal. Seconds later, two screaming boys landed in the chariot, but not in the back as usual. With a floppy jolt they landed in the front.

Zac shook his head to clear away the fright at realising they were on their own. Refocused, he took a hold of the reins that were flapping around in the breeze. 'We must be late?' He looked at the watch Ochimus gave him. 'No it seems we're on time?'

Bray had the NAVscan out of his pocket and was punching away at keys. 'Just let me see where we are.'

'Maybe Helios was worried we might not get to this mission on time and gave us a few more minutes,' Zac called to him over the sound of strained breathing. 'I think it's odd the horses are puffing and snorting like this. They're sluggish too. It's as if they've travelled for some distance before we arrived.'

'You're right on both accounts. We are almost at Venus,' said Bray.

They looked to the left of them where the horses diverted and had to shield their eyes. The clouds and debris that should have surrounded Venus were transparent. The planet was so bright due to the extreme heat. After the experience on Mercury, Bray took heed and now carried a safety kit.

His stepfather had spotted him trying to pack it at dinner time, tut-tutted him and gave him one similar to one he used as a lad. Bray didn't like to admit it to him, but the breathing mask he had given him had saved their lives on Mercury. With this in mind he was quite happy to toss the new one into his backpack before he left the house. It was this he dug around in and found two pairs of kooky sunglasses.

'Never seen this brand before.' Zac held them up, reading the label. 'NAVglow,' he read out before slipping them on. 'Your stepdad is starting to freak me out. These are incredible.'

Bray put his on. 'Holy moly!' He let out a

whistle. He was able to see through the cloud cover to Venus's surface. The mountains were coming up. They could see them clearly. 'Maxwell Ranges to the left.' Bray pointed.

Zac turned the horses. 'Which mountain do I head for? They all look the same height from up here.'

'Straight ahead. The one in the middle with a black tip,' Bray explained.

'Got it!' Zac was proficient in steering the horses. 'Do you want me to land them at the base on this side?'

'The artefact is just above us but straight ahead. That will be perfect.' Bray slipped the NAVscan back in his pocket as they landed with a jolt. He grabbed at the side of the chariot to hang on, both giving a chuckle at how much fun that was. 'You need a bit of practice with the landing Zac.' Bray was still having a dig at him as he opened the magic sack to see what was inside. He hoped all they needed was there. 'Cool!' He whistled as he pulled out ropes, nut, hexes and the endless stream of clothing, helmets and other protective gear.

'That bag is like Santa's sack.' Zac peered inside. 'It's small but stuff just keeps coming out.'

They put on the special tight clothing that covered them from head to toe. The soft chewy feeling shoes had a grip that stuck to the floor of the chariot. They could move their feet but the sensation was as if they had just stood on chewing gum. The balaclava type head gear was the hardest to get on. They had to stop and help each other as it was such a tight fit. But once on was very comfortable. It even had the same strange light material for around their eyes and mouth as their last suit. Only the material was a little different and felt almost spongy. Both were grateful for the Velcro tabs on each side to hold the NAVglow sunnies Eishol had given them. With the NAVglows back on, Bray didn't need his glasses. Looking out over the landscape he could see waves of heat in the atmosphere. It gave a similar vision to the water mirages those lost in a hot desert would see. Also the glow of this boiling, red-hot planet was made to look relatively normal through the special glass fitted into the trendy NAVglows.

'Bazinga! I can see perfectly.' Zac let out a wolf whistle. 'This planet is one sad ravaged place,' he said as he swung his head around to view the surface.

Finding the two small torches in his backpack, Bray handed one to Zac. He slid his own into the pouch of his belt. 'We should leave the backpack here,' Bray anguished, 'but what if we need something else?'

'The material might deteriorate.' Zac held it

up and as he did a spray can fell out of it and rolled onto the floor. He snatched it up before it rolled off the chariot and read the label. 'Material Heat Protectant spray. Coat material to protect garment from burning up in extreme heat conditions.' He looked at Bray. 'Where did this come from?'

Bray shrugged. 'Who cares? Let's use it.' He held the bag so Zac could give it a good soaking in the stuff. 'That should do it.' Bray gave the bag a shake.

'Well we can take it now,' Zac said as he helped Bray put it on his back. He dug around inside it, looking while he talked. 'You know Bray, I'd love to know where your stepfather found these glasses and now this can of heat resistant spray, but really, the rest of this safety kit is just regular issue. I bet it was a fluke he put those unusual items in. Let's not get all weird and start believing he knows about the quest we're on.'

'I guess you're right. He most likely got the safety gear from a second-hand joint. Maybe it belonged to some geeks like us, and these are experimental lab glasses or something. As for the spray...' Again he shrugged. 'He's one eccentric weirdo.' Bray lifted the rolled rope onto his shoulder. 'Gee the rope is so light, I bet they call it Navrope,' he smiled. The rest of the gear he had buckled neatly around his waist. 'Right to go?'

Adventures of Bray and Zac

'Sure am.' Zac did the same and then checked Bray's harness was buckled up correctly. He undid the clip and adjusted the straps for him before doing it back up. 'You're such a sloppy dresser Bray.' He grinned, unable to look at twisted straps.

'Thanks Mum,' Bray mocked him with a smile. He knew Zac was immaculate about everything; a quality Bray found annoying at first but was used to now.

Zac turned from him in a huff. 'So if you've finished hanging it on my safety side, can we get going?'

'Sorry Zac... Just a bit anxious about this planet. I know we have all the equipment we need. Just hope the batteries in the lights don't go flat before we get back. If we have to stumble around in the dark it will make it difficult to find our way back to the chariot.'

'Forgiven.' Zac imitated Bray turning on his hat lights.

'Let's go then. Get this expedition underway.' Bray slapped a hand on his back. 'Ready to rock climb?' He chuckled, trying to lighten the mood with a Bray-style joke.

'Sure am,' Zac agreed and followed him.

Both scampered over the side of the chariot

and headed off. Bray led the way, not at all worried about the climb ahead. He was pleased to note Zac looked forward to this mission too. There was a quirky smile on his lips that Bray had seen many times, always at the beginning of a new project. It was the anticipation and thrill of the journey ahead. He felt his face reflected this too. Bray's smile at Zac didn't go away and it was making his cheeks ache. But he couldn't switch it off.

'You know Zac...' he put an arm around him as they walked. 'We are the only Earthlings who have ever climbed this mountain on Venus.' He dropped his arm and walked with a spring in his step.

'Bray, buddy... That's because we are possibly the only humans that will ever come here, period.' The thought got Zac excited. He punched the air. 'We are so privileged.'

'Hope you're still that pumped when we're dangling from a cliff three hundred metres up.' Bray pointed upwards The hill they were to climb was steep, but luckily the shelf above them hid most of the mountain. He only had to look at Zac's face to see he had frightened him. 'Just kidding. Check it out, it doesn't look so bad, does it?' Bray said.

'G... guess not,' Zac stammered.

They stood at the bottom of the steep cliff.

It was time to concentrate on the next leg of their journey. Bray turned to his friend, whose breathing had become erratic. He tried to calm him as he linked their ropes. 'All that we learned at camp, the same applies here. We're doing a traditional rock climb so it won't be hard. We've done it before.'

'Remind me again?' Zac looked up. The colour had drained from his usually olive complexion. He was freaking out and they hadn't even started to move yet.

Taking this into account, Bray kept his tone light and happy. 'A traditional climb requires us to be partners so I'll be there with you the entire time. We are joined with this rope so you have to trust me that I won't stuff this up. You know I love outdoor camping, bushwalks, and especially rock climbing. Might be short, but my arms are strong.' He chuckled and playfully kissed his guns through his shirt.

It was what Zac needed and gave a laugh while he punched his arm. 'That may be so but I can run, you can't.'

Bray looked down at Zac's long legs that were hidden under the special protective gear he wore. 'Even through those I can see your chicken sticks. At least mine have shape.' Taking his mind off it, Bray started moving. Getting to the steep climb, he placed a nut and hex into the rock's crack. The next into the rock's spur. Zac followed, still going crook at him about the chicken leg comment. Bray was pleased they were given the correct harness. Soon they would be in a sitting position hanging in mid-air. This would give him free hands to work the rope. Keeping them both safe and sound was Bray's primary goal as he edged his way up the rugged mountain cliff. Although entertaining, he broke in on Zac's insults. Gunnar-boy, nitwit was the last of them. 'Okay need your help now Zac. You have to start feeding me extra rope through the belay device.' He pointed to the connection.

'I know what it is Bray.' He rolled his eyes.

'Sorry Zac, just checking. You okay now?'

'I guess so.' He looked down. 'Gee whiz, I didn't think we were this high up.'

Bray started moving. 'Keep up the name calling. It's amusing and so long as it keeps your mind off the climb, I'm all for it.'

He looked back down again. 'Nah I'm good now. You got me this far and I'm still alive so I guess I can start trusting you.' He gave Bray the thumbs up. 'Go for it!'

As soon as he had Zac's approval, Bray really started to put his back into it and scampered up the cliff, Zac only just keeping up with him.

Bray suddenly stopped. The peg he put in place broke away. He tried again.

It mucked up Zac's momentum. 'What's going on?' Heavy breathing from both boys sounded loud in the silent darkness. The hat Zac wore shone light to see what was going on. 'You have the peg thing in, so let's move Bray! We only have an hour left of our allotted climb. After that we better start descending or we'll never get back in time.'

'I know!' Bray sounded as panicked. 'This rock won't hold us both. It's a bit weak. But I've found a crack that seems to be holding fast. I'm just using it to swing me across to that boulder.' He pointed to one about three metres away. 'Just hang tight. And don't follow me until I say.'

'What! You think I'm an ape? No way am I doing... that!' Zac hissed.

'I have you tightly secured. And don't think this alien rope is made light just for us to carry. I reckon it's strong enough to hold an ox up here.'

'Well, be careful. If that peg gives way you will land on me.'

'I doubt that it will but in case it does, best get ready to catch me!' Bray called out as he swung back and forth getting momentum enough to reach the rock.

'Drat, I missed.' Bray called out. 'I'm going again.' As he kicked off the rock, the peg slipped in the crack between the rocks and Bray dropped with a jerking motion.

'Careful Bray... jeepers.' Zac had his hand to his mouth feeling frightened for him.

Not about to give up that easily, Bray wiggled the peg and feeling it was secure, swung back and forth again, building a momentum.

'Phew!' His hand gripped the cavity he aimed for and he didn't let it go until he had secured himself firmly to it.

'Your turn,' he called to Zac. 'It held me, so it will most definitely hold your skinny bag of bones.' He joked to keep Zac from overthinking it and possibly losing confidence.

After much coaching, Zac began his swing towards Bray. It was a good one and Bray caught him on the second go. 'Glad you plucked up the guts, I need you to be brave. What got you moving?' He secured Zac to him. At this point they were both suspended in mid-air.

'Decided it's better to die trying, rather than die on this planet because we missed the chariot.'

'Good plan and guess what.' Bray had pulled the NAVscan out of his pocket.

Adventures of Bray and Zac

'What?' Zac squinted to see what he was on about.

'All we have to do is pull ourselves up the rope. Once over the other side of this rock we'll be on the ledge and we're there.'

'Wahoo! Hang on. If you knew we were almost there, why not leave my whining self where it was and go get it alone?'

'No way Zac, we do this together... all the way. That hero swing we both just did proves we can do this. We make a good team don't you reckon?'

'Yes... but you weren't scared?'

'You think! That was for sure, the scariest thing I've ever had to do. I pretended it was easy so you'd do it to. But phew... I nearly shat myself.'

'I think I did.' Zac let out a nervous chuckle.

'Guts got us here, motivation to get back in time, or die, will give us the courage we need to get back down.' Sweat poured from Bray's forehead, as he worried they had taken more time than he'd calculated. Once they got up to the ledge above, six hours would have passed. That meant they had only two hours to get back to their ride home. He was glad they had been given an extra fifteen minutes by being transported directly into the chariot already en route.

The two of them worked like clockwork together, best friends in sync. Both high fived one another once they finally reached the artefact box.

'Great job!' Zac praised Bray.

'Same to you.' Bray was amazed they got up there with no other incidents. 'What have we here?' He bent down to eye off the ancient carvings on the box. He brushed off the black ash that covered it. 'I wonder if we should be taking note of what's written on these boxes?' He pulled off his backpack. 'I'm sure I have pen and paper. We can sketch it.'

'We haven't much time. And it's so hot here the paper would burn. What about the NAVscan? Does it take pictures?'

'Not sure, let me have a look.' Bray shrugged and typed in camera. Sure enough the image changed and he was looking at the ground. 'Cool!' He hit the button that came up and *"saved"* popped up. 'Ancient markings on artefact now recorded.' He turned it to show Zac.

'That means we have to go back to Mercury.' Zac slapped a hand to his head. 'How could we have missed that clue?' The stress in his voice made him sound almost hysterical.

Bray had to calm him down. After Mercury,

Adventures of Bray and Zac

they had both agreed the witch there had scared the bejeezers out of them. But he needed to be positive for Zac's sake. 'Let's wait till we get home and decrypt it. We still have our challenges here and this expedition isn't over yet.' He looked around. 'We have to work out yet how to get off this mountain in record time.' He smiled as he saw Zac's tense shoulders relax.

'You're right! Let's open this thing and get out of here!' He dropped quickly to his knees beside Bray. 'Let me help you pull out the box. It came out easier last time, with both of us tugging at it.'

But even both of them pulling at it, didn't budge the artefact from the rocks it was wedged between. It didn't take long before they realised the first time was a fluke. Half an hour later they sat down on the ground, exhausted.

'What are we doing differently?' Zac slumped over, his elbow resting on his knees, head in hands.

Bray studied the markings on the NAVscan. 'That has to be it.' He leant towards Zac. The picture enlarged and they could see clearly a button. 'Bet that's it.' He leant over and pressed it. The box, as last time, slid from its cavity and opened.

Zac snatched it up. 'Got it. Nice work.' He grinned at his friend.

The Magic Portal

Bray saw he had it and jumped up. He knew they had to get a wriggle on. Bray put out his hand and helped him to his feet. The rocks were slippery and it took Zac a second to get his footing.

'These suits need better grip on the feet. Remind me to tell Helios next we meet.' Zac cursed as he nearly slipped again.

Bray did a funny jig. 'Mine are fine. It's this height playing tricks with your equilibrium. Here, hold this rope. I'll get you down as quick as I can and you'll feel a lot better. This'll be close.'

'Unless you are going to fly us down, I can't see us getting off here any time soon.' Zac scowled.

Bray smiled while he took the other rolled up rope from Zac's backpack. If he'd told Zac before that they were abseiling he would have freaked out.

'Watch grasshopper and learn.' He chuckled, lifted the hammer and brought it down hard onto the anchor points he held in place. Once firmly embedded in the rock he attached the two ropes, double checking to make sure both ends were tightly secured.

'What do I do?' Zac watched on with a pout. He hated it when Bray knew what to do and didn't share, but was starting to figure it out and was not happy about it. 'I know what you want me to do Bray, but let me tell you, you're crazy if you think

I'm following you to your death.'

'Stop being melodramatic Zac. I need you to take a chill pill and follow my lead. See this rope? All you have to hold it Zac. The combination of your weight and gravity will drive you downwards. Yes, we are up high, but remember the training we had. It's no different to that, only we will rappel down a lot faster.' Bray demonstrated. 'Hold your rope firm like this and get your footing, then simply kick off from the wall.'

Zac settled in beside him. As scared as he was he didn't want to stay up there alone. 'Okay, I think I remember. But it was only a quick lesson and only off an indoor rock wall.'

'I know buddy. But we have no other choice. We can do this together. You ready?'

Zac took a deep breath. 'Ready as I'll ever be!'

'Good! And no stopping once we start. And Zac,' he made a hand gesture. 'Eyes on me, or up. No looking down. On three! One ... Two... Three.' Bray counted and waited for Zac to kick off first and was one second behind his every landing, encouraging him all the way down. It was on the second last jump that Bray gave him instructions as to what they would do when they hit the ground. 'Unclip yourself and run at full speed. You will be heady from coming down so fast, but fight through the haze when your feet touch the ground. We will have little time to make it to the chariot. Just give it all you've got and run, Zac. Run like you have never run before!'

Zac gave him thumbs up.

Both hit the ground simultaneously.

'We have four minutes... Run!' Bray screamed out as they helped each other free of the clasps that held them like spiders to a web. Both took off at full speed. This was not Bray's forte and over pushing it to keep up to Zac, he face planted onto the dirt. It was Zac's turn to save his pal and he skidded to a halt, and went back to help him up. His protective suit had sliced open on the rough gravel and Bray started to scream from the burn he was receiving through the slight split. Not giving it any thought, Zac threw him over his wide shoulders and ran.

The horses must have known something was up and ran towards them. Zac threw Bray over into the chariot and had time only to hold on to the outside of it as the horses took off into the air.

Bray collected himself now in the protection of the chariot. Alert again he heard the screams from Zac. 'Would you like a hand?' Bray reached over the side of the cart and grabbed Zac's arm to help him in. 'Geez, it seems I'm always the one saving your arse.'

Both landed heavily on the floor of the chariot. Zac punched Bray in the arm. 'You always saving me!' Then he saw Bray was joking and both busted up laughing.

Zac stopped laughing and looked straight at the burn on Bray's leg. 'Are you okay buddy?'

'All joking aside, you saved my life Zac. I'm so grateful.'

'You just saved mine. We're even. But glad you appreciated it. You're one heavy sucker to run with.' Zac grinned and nudged him. 'Someone has to drive the horses. You want me to?' Zac hoped Bray would let him.

'Go for it. I'm going to get out of this suit and see if Eishol has put burn cream in my bag,' said Bray

They both sat up and struggled out of the alien protective clothing. To take any of the safety gear home would be too hard to explain if found by inquisitive parents.

Once Bray attended to his burn and put a bandage around it, he sat up front with Zac. 'We did it... together.' Bray put an arm around his buddy's shoulders. Dressed in his own clothes and not in pain, he felt normal again.

The Magic Portal

'Yep, we did it!' Zac nudged his arm off as he always did. He hated affection. 'There's no need to get all huggy.' Zac wasn't sure why but he squirmed at compliments. 'I would have done that for anyone.'

Bray knew that was crap. Zac had saved him many times against bullies, to a point where he became the victim too, as he had done the previous day at school against Grogan. This chivalry had him standing in his undies in front of the entire school only yesterday. He ignored the remark. Never had he seen Zac even attempt to "save" anyone else. Bray believed his dislike of affection was his parents' doing. They were never home. His upbringing was virtually left to his big sister. He never understood Zac's parents.

Bray's own mum was the total opposite, to the point of embarrassing as she hugged him so often. Bray was just glad she was mad at him right now. Otherwise he would never be able to escape as he had been doing.

He shuddered, remembering the kiss on the cheek she would request for driving him to school, in front of his friends... eeek. If only she knew of the toilet dunking after being caught by school bullies. But this eight day challenge had begun to change both of them.

The fear of being transported into the

immortal world had them hold on tight to each other. Both screamed during the process because it was so frightening, but they never discussed backing out. Bray wondered if they both might come through this, new and improved. Maybe one day they might put Grogan's clothes in the tree and leave him standing in his undies... he smiled at the happy thought.

Both sat contemplating, relieved this task was over. They were shocked that although still classed as kids, they had climbed that mountain they looked down upon.

They lost focus on it as the horses flew higher in the night sky and so engrossed in memories, neither noticed the atmosphere fog up. With hoarse voices from fear and weariness they cried out for each other, locking arms as the force of magic spun them around and around. The wind tunnel that sparked lightning bolts, tossed them onto the floor in Zac's room... *splat!* They landed with force. Both rubbed their backsides, sore from the fall. Scrambling to their feet they fist pumped with a gesture of fists exploding.

'We made it. Night two ... tick,' Bray said.

'Remind me to drag my mattress on the floor tonight before we leave. Those landings are a buzz kill,' Zac said as he rubbed his tender spots from the heavy landing as he sat at the computer.

'You need more meat on your bones Zac.' Bray chuckled as he sat in the chair next to him. 'Okay, where to next, bud?'

'Earth!' Zac kept searching as he spoke. 'Wonder if the horses will be invisible.'

'Good point,' Bray said while he straightened his shirt. 'Imagine the chariot being invisible and us not. How funny will it look?' He stopped as his joke fell on deaf ears. Zac had tuned out on him, engrossed in reading what was on the screen. 'What you looking at?' Bray squinted and pulled a chair close to Zac so he could see the screen. 'Are you doing a search to see if our artefact has already been found?'

'Yes,' Zac said, and pointed. 'It says here that the oldest artefact ever found, was discovered in Gona, Ethiopia. It's said to be close to 2.6 million years old.'

'Amazing, but not what we are looking for,' said Bray.

'At least we know it's still in the ground.' Zac turned to Bray.

Bray pulled out the NAVscan. 'Let's see where we're heading. If it has magically moved itself to the surface like the others we need to find it and quick.' Bray moved his finger lightly across the touch screen to bring up the much needed

Adventures of Bray and Zac

information.

'Too right! I agree, before someone else does.'

Bray looked up, unable to concentrate with the thought of someone else finding it if it had surfaced, but after staring into thin air, he shrugged. 'I vote we worry about that scenario if it happens.' Bray continued putting in the planet, in this case Earth, and pressed the button that said "locate".

'It's here!' He jumped from his seat and punched the air. 'Yahoo! No chariot needed. We can take our bikes... tonight if you're up to it.'

Zac stood. 'Really! Where!' He sounded just as excited.

'Down by the old mine. You know the one... we got into trouble big time for playing there as kids.'

'That's right, grounded for a month.' Zac chuckled. 'Well... they didn't lock our windows, so it was kind of a grounding... not.'

Bray held the NAVscan in front of Zac as he talked. 'See. Half an hour's bike ride and we can play hooky tomorrow from school and leisurely study the forth planet, Mars.'

'Have a good sleep, sounds wonderful.' Zac

grinned at him.

'And after wagging school tomorrow, we will be refreshed and ready to tackle big red.' Bray gave a snorty laugh, thinking he was funny.

'You mean Mars,' Zac corrected him with a straight face.

'What I said, big red.'

Zac didn't get it. 'Bray it's one of the smaller planets.'

'I know... that's the joke.' He snorted and laughed again.

Zac got it finally and flashed Bray one of those big toothy grins. 'You're so lame,' he said, and nudged Bray. 'Sleep deprivation is making me laugh at anything.' He chuckled too but more at Bray snorting than anything else.

Chapter Seven

Earth

They had both grabbed their backpacks, bikes and a torch, as Bray didn't have lights on his bike. This was a mission they chose to do on their own.

'Earth mission is a go!' Bray called out.

They had been riding on blacktop surface for some time before the NAVscan beeped. 'We veer off onto this dirt track. This is the back way to the coal mine entrance.' Bray turned to Zac who followed, looking up.

'Check out the moon, Bray.' Zac put up his hand and pointed to it. 'It's shining so brightly. We don't need our lights on anymore.'

Zac flicked his bike light off and at the same time, Bray turned off the slimline light he was using and slipped it into his pocket. 'This is going to be

Adventures of Bray and Zac

the easiest find of them all. I'm stoked. What do you think buddy?'

'Shush. I can hear talking,' Zac whispered.

'Me too.' Bray stopped beside Zac who pulled up in front of him. It was lucky they had turned their light off a little way back; it had prevented them being seen. They quietly wheeled the bikes behind some bushes and pulled the spiny branches over to camouflage them. They could not risk the bikes being found. They were the only means of transport to get them home. There were three boys standing over something. As they crept closer, they saw it was the bully Grogan from school and a couple of his goony mates. They had found the artefact box and were trying to access it. Bray had no other choice but to confront them.

'Stay here!' he whispered and stopped Zac from joining him. 'I might need your help to get me out of a tree or something if this doesn't work.'

Zac didn't look happy but backed up and hid in an old cart. Here he waited and anxiously watched. He couldn't hear much of what was said but saw Grogan had sent his boys looking for him.

Unable to find Zac they went back to Grogan. He slapped one of them across the head. Zac figured it was for not doing as he asked. Then he grabbed Bray by the neck of his T-shirt and lifted him. He held Bray at arm's length. His short legs were suddenly off the ground. Bray kicked furiously but not one connected with the bully. Zac panicked and looking around saw Grogan's dirt motorbike and the second rusty heap of rubbish that the other two must have piggy backed on. He glanced over at one stage and saw Bray pull something from his coat pocket, spraying it in Grogan's face first, then turning it on the other two boys. Zac smirked when he realised it was something disgusting. He could also smell it and pulled his shirt up over his nose. He had to work fast; it looked as if they would be making a run for it. Just as he finished his own delaying tactics he heard Bray yelling out at the top of his lungs. Zac glanced over. The three boys Bray sprayed were rolling around on the dirt shouting abuse trying to rub off the stench. Bray ran past them, jumping high to prevent Grogan grabbing his ankle.

'Zac... RUN! BIKES!' he cried out.

At the bikes, and at record pace, they uncovered their pushbikes and jumped on them. They pumped their legs hard to pick up speed.

They hadn't gone far when they heard two motorbikes start up.

'Oh crap!' said Bray. 'Didn't know they had motorbikes. How can we out-ride them? Please tell me you have a plan.'

Zac turned to him. 'Just pedal like hell and hope my sabotage works. And what the hell did you spray on them?'

'Another stepdad thing. Never thought I'd use that skunk spray, but did you see how well that stuff worked? Those dudes stink.' He looked back, his eyes like saucers. 'If those bullies catch me though, I'm dead.'

'Did you get the artefact?' Zac asked as they turned onto the main road. He was hoping someone would come along and help them before the bikes caught up to them.

'Sure did. But maybe we should head for the bushes beside us. Stop and hide.'

'Trust me. We are safer running. Now pedal faster!' Zac commanded.

Wheels squealed on asphalt alerting them before they even heard the insults and abuse from Grogan and his goons. They were right behind them.

'There's no one around; we're dead, Zac. I hate my stepdad for making me carry that stuff.' Bray cried. 'But he was hurting me. I had no choice.'

'This is life or death for humanity, Bray. He will forgive you next week after he realises we saved him and everyone else. Focus and pedal as

The Magic Portal

hard as you can.' Zac could hear the bike motors coming up beside them.

All of a sudden there was a loud grinding sound and bang, and then the other went just after it. Grogan had his hand out ready to rip Bray off his treadly when his bike backfired again and the motor stalled. The bike came to an abrupt stop not very far from the first.

'What was that?' Bray swivelled in his seat to take a glimpse behind him. Grogan waved his fist at them, his words drowned out by the sound of them trying to kick the bike motors back to life. Bray noticed Zac had a big grin when they both turned to the road ahead. 'What did you do?'

'Well they are dirt bikes, right. I thought they ran on dirt. Oops, must be mistaken. Didn't have any fuel to give them.'

'Oh we are so dead.' Bray shook his head. 'Glad we're not going to school today.'

Chapter Eight

PLANETARIUM

Home in bed, Bray lay back with his hands locked behind his head, and a big smile beamed out. He had stood up to Grogan. The schoolyard bully had terrorised him all through school and for once he had got the upper hand. He knew he would get a bollocking when he went back to school, but tonight he was pumped. He was excited there were ways to beat a beast of a bully like him, even if it did take skunk spray to subdue him. He drifted off to sleep, and the smile lingered.

Next morning, Bray told Eishol, Zac's sister was taking them to school. Eishol surprised Bray and left for work leaving him alone. Bray pulled the covers over his head and went back to sleep. It was 3pm when he struggled out of bed. He had slept all day and only got up because his stepdad usually came home around 3.30pm. Bray worked this out because Eishol had always arrived at school to pick him up looking as if he had just showered and changed. This was the reason Bray didn't know what work he did. Bray's plan was simple. He would have a shower, and get dressed as though he had been to school. Once he heard the front door open he would come out of his room saying he was let out of school early.

The plan was interrupted when he came out of his room and to his surprise, Eishol sat on a stool in the kitchen. 'You're home early son.' He had a half grin.

It made Bray cross. He hated him calling him *son*. Plus his well thought out plan had failed. 'You know I wagged. So go tell Mum. I don't care.' He pushed his glasses up on his nose. 'And I've told you before, I'm not your son.' He picked up his backpack to leave and go over the road to Zac's.

'It's a figure of speech. Come on Bray. I'm sorry.' Eishol turned towards him and crossed his arms. 'Where are you off to young man?'

'Going to Zac's,' he muttered. 'Unless you're here to gloat and ground me, I'm out of here.'

'Hang on. When did I become your mum? You can do as you please. I'm just helping out your mum by watching out for you. I knew you would sleep in if I wasn't here to wake you, so I came home early to see if you wanted to go to the Planetarium to help with your studies. You've done nothing but chat to your mum about your project, and I thought this is something we could do together.'

'Why?' Bray asked with suspicion.

'I too study the planets, sort of. Well, I build satellites that study them. I work with NASA.'

Bray blinked, surprised. 'Really!'

'You can bring your friend from across the way. That is of course if it wouldn't bore you both. Studying the planets and stars is not for everyone.' His stepdad shrugged.

'I'll go get Zac.' He took off, not looking at him.

'Good. I'll pick you up out the front of Zac's in five minutes, so no dawdling.'

'Okay,' Bray called back. Sounding out a loud, 'Yahoo!' he hit the lawn and jumped high in the air, excited.

Zac heard Bray's voice and pulled the curtain back. Seeing Bray running towards his house, he hung his head out the window from the second floor up. 'What's going on? Have you gone mad?' he called down to Bray who had almost reached his door.

Bray looked up. 'Wanna go to the

Planetarium?'

'Well yes! Hell yes! When do we leave?' Zac hung out of the window. Half in... half out... he kept his friend in sight.

'Five minutes.'

'Who's taking us?' Zac asked.

'Eishol.' His smile left him and he shrugged. 'Whatever, at least we get to go there. Mum promised but never got around to it. So my stepdad will do hey!'

'Sure will. I'm starting to like that dude!' He grinned widely. 'Come on up. Door's open. I've just had a shower and will throw on some clobber.'

'Oh no!' Bray looked down, went inside and started jogging up the stairs towards Zac's room. 'Got a t-shirt for me? Put this school shirt on to fool my stepdad, but turns out he's on to me.'

'Can't fool him like you do your mum.' Zac tossed him a shirt as soon as he was in sight. 'Your favourite, but I want it back.'

'Superheros – you sure?'

'Feeling generous. After all, you have organised a great way for us to check out the rest of the planets we need to visit. You're the coolest.'

The Magic Portal

From inside, they heard the rumble of Eishol's car turn into the driveway. 'He's here. Ready?' Bray shoved his school shirt in his bag and slung it over his shoulder.

'Coming!' Zac was right behind him.

At the planetarium, Bray looked for the perfect seats where they would get the best views.

'Sit here!' Bray threw himself back in his chosen seat. Zac and Eishol sat either side of him.

Zac leaned back, his eyes wide with excitement. 'Wow, look at this place. It's huge.' Zac turned his face towards Bray and his stepdad. 'I'm so glad you let me tag along. I've heard so much about the planetarium, but the folks were always too busy to bring me.'

'Wait until the lights go down and the show starts.' Eishol stood up. 'I'll leave you boys to it. Just need to duck out and make a phone call. Save my seat.'

'Sure.' Bray turned to him. He couldn't wipe the smile off his face. He was psyched Eishol had brought them, but even more thrilled to find he wasn't hanging around the entire time. He and Zac had stuff to discuss and didn't want *him* around

ADVENTURES OF BRAY AND ZAC

listening. He turned straight back to Zac, ignoring further babble that didn't interest him. 'Whatever.' Bray had tuned out and began a new conversation with Zac. 'Hey, did you see the detail of the moon out there? Wish we were being sent there on a mission.'

Zac nodded. 'And what about when we got to see Neil Armstrong's suit! I'd never have climbed that hill on Venus in that thing. Glad Helios is looking out for us. We get such cool gear compared to Earth astronauts.'

'I wish Eishol wasn't with us out there. I wanted to say that too. I'm so pumped I could hardly keep my gob shut.' Bray chuckled with Zac.

The lights went down.

'It's about to begin,' Zac punched Bray when he snorted with more laughter. 'Shush! You nut.' He muffled his own joy. Then he looked upwards. It had begun. Above them was the illusion of the universe on a clear night. Stars twinkled above in the cloudless sky. He turned his head towards Bray. 'Thanks for bringing me along. This is the best time ever.'

Bray grinned. 'The coolest...' His words were silenced by powerful imagery and sound as the planet they needed to learn about came into view. When Mars was focused on, the boys were

The Magic Portal

so preoccupied with the details about the planet, they didn't even hear Eishol come back and sit with them.

'Look at how small Mars is beside Jupiter,' Zac pointed out.

'And it's so red,' said Bray.

They sat quietly listening to why. Both glanced at each other when they learned it was the iron-rich minerals in the soil and rock that gave it the crust the red rust colour. And that the red planet is home to the highest mountain.

'That Olympus Mons on Mars is three times taller than Mount Everest. Did you know, Mars also has the deepest, longest valley in the solar system. The Marineris system of valleys was named after the Mariner 9 probe that discovered it in 1971,' Bray whispered.

'How do you know that?' Zac whispered back.

'In the foyer I read a brochure while you were checking out the two satellite photos of the two moons above Mars.' Bray kept his voice low so not to disturb anyone. 'The Valleys can go as deep as 10 km and run for roughly 4,000 km. Hope the artefact's not buried there.' Bray paused as the music stopped and talking began again. He was surprised when he heard Mars also had the largest volcanoes in the solar system, including Olympus Mons, being approximately 600 km in diameter.

Zac whistled between his teeth. 'That's wide enough to cover the entire state of New Mexico. Hope it isn't there either.'

The show continued, with the boys happy to hear Mars has seasons. ...*Away from the sun, the surface carbon dioxide causes snow clouds to form in the atmosphere. In winter, watery ice snow falls from these clouds dropping surface temperature from: -5 to -87 °C.*

They turned to each other.

Zac grinned. 'Better than burning to death on Venus.'

'Agree.' Bray nodded.

Then both boys slumped in their seats when the speaker told them of dust storms capable of blanketing the entire red planet and last for months. It continued, saying how strong winds apparently lift dust off the ground, which in turn heats the atmosphere, creating more wind and kicking up more dust.

'Well I hope we don't have to contend with too much dust,' said Bray. 'I'll do nothing but sneeze with my allergies.'

'You know I hate dust too,' Zac agreed. 'But

not because of allergies. I just don't like getting dirty, as you well know.' He shuddered.

The show ended. 'I thought we would learn about all the Planets,' Bray said and jumped when Eishol spoke.

'That's it for the day boys. We missed the full show which was earlier. But I was betting Mars was what you would have learned at school today so made sure I was home in time to bring you here. Can't have this strange project you boys are working on fail for want of some information. You study well into the night so I guessed it must be important to you.'

'Thanks Mr. ... err...' Zac wasn't sure what his surname was. Bray must know, but Bray hated talking about him.

'Just call me Eishol.' He stood. 'Well, I better get you boys back. It's getting late. We'll grab some takeaway on the trip home. How's that sound?'

'It's only 6.30. Mum won't care if we are a bit late,' Bray said.

'Oh, forgot to tell you. I'm taking your mum out for dinner tonight. I was going to drop you at home with Zac unless you are sick of each other by now. You can come with us if you want, Bray.'

'No! Don't worry about me.' Bray didn't

want to sit looking at Eishol across the dinner table after spending the afternoon with him. *Stepdad overload.* 'I'm happy to be dropped off at Zac's. We both have to write up what we just learned and enter it into our project notes. We may as well do it while it's fresh in our minds,' Bray said.

Chapter Nine

Mars

At Zac's they sat cross legged eating Asian meat and noodles from a box. Neither coordinated enough to use the chopsticks supplied, they ate with their fingers. Both talked with their mouths full, spitting it everywhere as they joyfully went over their trip to the Planetarium. They laughed hard how Eishol was so gullible. They'd both maintained they had no money so he not only paid their entry into the Planetarium, but shouted snacks and dinner.

Zac stopped laughing and attempted to stick up for Eishol. 'He tries, Bray. You should try to be nicer to him.'

'Well he shouldn't be such a sticky beak. I mean all those questions on the way home! As if we would tell – him – what we are doing every night. He is so annoying.' Fingers disappeared into Bray's box of noodles. The thick sauce ran down his chin

Adventures of Bray and Zac

as he fed them into his mouth. Slowly chewing, he came up with another topic to steer the subject away from his *stupid* stepdad.

'Hey! What's with the moons above Mars having names?' Bray switched the subject.

'Only ours is called a moon. Theirs are called Phobos and Deimos.' Zac smiled. 'Phobos means fear and Deimos means panic. They were named after the horses that pulled the chariot of the Greek war god Ares.'

'He must still live on Mars somewhere? I'm betting if Helios exists, so would Ares,' Bray surmised.

Zac agreed and continued. He enjoyed telling Bray something for once he didn't know. 'And... they are not only tiny compared to our moon, but not perfectly round,' Zac said.

'Why?' Bray kept him talking.

'They lack the gravity ours has to pull them into a more circular shape.' Zac tossed his empty noodle box in the bin by his desk and missed, shrugged and sipped on his drink. 'Oh, nearly forgot, Phobos is spiralling toward Mars. It moves 1.8 meters closer to the red planet each century. The astronomers believe that in 50 million years, Phobos may smash into Mars. That, or break apart and the smashed rock will form a ring around the planet.'

Bray grinned. 'I knew all that. Just wanted to get you off the subject of my stepdad.'

'Loser!' Zac pushed him and Bray rolled onto his side, spilling the rest of his sauce.

'Good one Zac. I was enjoying that.'

'Here, you can have my chocolate bar.' He tossed it to Bray and stood up. 'I've had plenty. Want to crank up the tower and check out where we are going tomorrow night? So glad we have a break tonight. Going to enjoy some much needed sleep.'

They had been studing the magic book but before they could lock it away it bounced off the desk and opened up.

Bray checked his watch. 'Boy oh boy it's eight o'clock. But we did Earth last night. What's it doing?' He grabbed his backpack and slipped his arms through the straps. Zac helped him buckle it.

'Better hold on, buddy,' said Bray, 'we are going somewhere whether we want to or not.' The room filled of mist and their bodies began to lift of the ground.

Zac searched the room for the NAVscan. On snatching it up he handed it to Bray. His eyes were wide as he reached out with his left hand and grabbed for Bray's shoulder.

'Ouch.' Bray winced as fingers dug into his flesh.

'Br — ay! So — rry.' Zac yelled out knowing it was he who caused Bray to feel pain. Even so, he clutched his friend as they circled the air above the book. He gulped back cries of distorted weirdness as they were sucked into the book. *Thump! Thump!* They landed in the chariot. Both wide-eyed, they looked around to see where they were. The chariot was motionless and Helios nowhere in sight.

'Well this is strange. We're in front of Helios's home, but where are he and his son? The horses are puffing so they've only just pulled up.' Bray was reluctant to get out the chariot. He was getting prickles up his spine as if something was very wrong.

'I wonder where the bull-men are who normally tend to the horses.' Zac pulled his brows in tight. 'It's too quiet, Bray. I don't like this at all.'

'I agree.' Bray put his hands to each side of his mouth. 'Hello!' he called out.

The loudness of his voice spooked the horses

that were still attached to the chariot. They flew up in the air. The action had both boys hang on tight.

'It doesn't feel right with me, Bray.' Zac spoke through gritted teeth. He was only barely hanging on as they moved so quickly.

'Me either,' Bray called out over the puffing of the horses. 'And you're right! On our first visit to Helios's home, the bull men come to attend these prize steeds as soon as they landed.'

'What's happening now?' Zac glanced down to see where the horses intended to land.

The horses flew back to where they had been and came to a halt. Once again, there was not a servant or horseman in sight.

'Where is everyone? It looks deserted.' Bray stood up and this time spoke little more quietly so as not to spook the horses again. He stood on tippy toes to see if he could spot anyone around the grounds of Helios's home.

'What's going on here?' Zac jumped to his feet now the chariot was still again. He looked just as confused. 'We shouldn't be here. Mars is not until tomorrow night.' He also spoke quietly.

'Let's go see?' Zac lifted his leg over the chariot to find it hit a wall or something. He put his hands against the invisible wall and pressed hard but could not penetrate it.

Bray copied the action on his side. Next he tried to get out the end of the chariot but found whatever direction they went in the invisible wall prevented them getting off. 'Okay this is really weird. Maybe we are meant to ride the horses somewhere, Zac.'

Zac picked up the reins and gave them a good flick. The horses flew up high and headed toward the sky. They turned left and zig zagged around some debris before they levelled out and flew straight ahead.

'Guess you're right Bray. The horses are taking us somewhere. I have no control on which way they are turning.' He let the reins go loose in his hands. Struggling to control their direction was hopeless.

'I'll see where we are headed.' Bray plucked out the NAVscan from his pocket. He pointed it to the northern part of the sky to reset it. 'Hey! We're on a course to... Mars! But we don't have to go there until tomorrow night.'

Zac called to the horses. 'Hey, horses! You mucked up. Mars is tomorrow night. Do you under-stand.' But that got not even a head shake. 'Turn around. Seriously we want to go home!' His voice sounded high pitched as they disobeyed the pull on the reins he usually used to turn them around. He called to them by name, 'Pyrios, Aeos, Aethon and Phlegon, turn around and go back home.' Still they flew forward. Their wings had been gently gliding, but calling their names only caused their great wings to stretch out farther and flap hard. Their legs galloped as if they were on land. In the sky it looked almost funny. They used every bit of power to get them moving quickly. 'I don't get it.' He glanced at Bray before looking back at the horses.

Bray moved over and stood next to him. 'Something's strange about this whole night. Let's relax and see what happens next. Maybe we're invited for supper if we get back early enough.' He kidded.

'But where was everyone back at the planet?' Zac frowned.

Bray shrugged. 'Beats me?'

Zac shook his head. 'This is just not right.'

'Well we're here now. So we best buckle up buddy and unwind. This is going to be one unplanned recovery. See... Look for yourself.' He pointed into the back of the chariot.

'What, we have no gear!' Zac squeaked out.

'That's correct Zac. No gear... he has left us

to rough this recovery. Glad we got my backpack on in time.'

'Lucky Eishol saw you left it in the car and called you back,' said Zac.

'I saw him zipping it up. Bet he was taking a look at what I had used,' said Bray.

'Or maybe he put something in it,' Zac suggested.

'Let's take a look.' Bray unclipped the catch that secured the bag to him and slipped it from his shoulders. He sat with it on the floor between his knees, unzipped it and pulled out what had been stuffed in it by Eishol.

'OMG, he knows.' Zac knelt beside him.

'Careful Zac, you're meant to be steering the horses,' Bray panicked.

'Be blowed, they aren't listening to me at all tonight. Look, I'm still holding the reins.' He pulled them to the left but the horses kept going straight ahead. He shrugged. 'Maybe they will let me land them.'

Bray grinned. 'I'm sure they will. Hey, thanks for not losing it tonight. I need you to do what you always do, stay calm for me. It keeps me from losing it. Everything is so weird. Even this.' Bray held up two pairs of glasses. They were different from the last ones his stepdad stashed in his bag.

Zac smiled his big gawky grin, making Bray laugh. After, he looked at what Bray held he agreed. 'He knows doesn't he?'

Bray lifted the goggles to his eyes. 'These are slightly different but I'm sure they have the same glass in them...'

'Like the ones we used on Venus. Those ones helped us see through the scorching waves of heat.' Zac finished off his sentence.

'Exactly, but I lost them when we were swept back home,' said Bray

'How would he know that unless he went through your bag? He's been snooping. And why would we need them on Mars. Yes it's a red planet but only in colour.'

'Agree. But let's check the temperature here.' Bray punched coordinates into the NAVscan and held it up to Zac. 'This blows that theory buddy. The artefact is there, right on the equator. It's showing 20°C. So no! He doesn't know anything. He is just trying hard to win me over or has OCD when it comes to safety.' Bray placed them down on his lap. He turned the bag upside down and gave it a good shake. The rest of the contents spilled out onto the chariot floor. Now he was able to see it better.

Zac shuffled through things too. 'What's with the gardening tools? Does he think we tend to the garden at night?' He laughed. 'Okay I'm definitely wrong about him for sure.'

Bray laughed too. 'Told you. But these aren't garden tools, this is espionage gear. And look at this other stuff. This looks like you would use it to pick a lock, there's a miniature fire extinguisher, two lightweight fire blankets and a burns kit. Oh and breathing masks. Hello, we don't need any of this gear. He has no idea of our mission, that I am positively sure. As you know we're protected from heat and below zero degree temperatures if we stay within specified metres of the chariot. Well, the exception being left behind on a planet. But that won't be happening tonight as the artefact looks like for once it's in clear view with nothing surrounding the box. Easy pick up and we are homebound.'

'Wow lucky us. Plus it's daytime on Mars. We don't even need torches and the weather sounds perfect,' Zac added.

'I reckon that's why we have nothing this time. We won't need the safety gear because this mission will be straight in and straight out. Easy peasy,' said Bray.

'It will be a change to be back in bed by midnight. Yahoo!' Zac yelled. His excited yelp was lost in Bray's whistle.

'Zac! The reins. We have arrived.'

Zac jumped to his feet and looked out over the sky, as the red planet came up fast. 'Where do I land?'

Bray had sprung up beside him and holding the NAVscan he pointed. 'There, head for that big mountain.'

'Isn't that Mount Olympus, that really old volcano we learned about?' Zac yelled over the noise of something happening on the surface.

'Sure is. It's almost three times the height of Mount Everest back home.' He had to yell too.

'What's all this in the air, where's it coming from?' Zac suddenly found it hard to see. He blinked and squinted through the black ash that poured from the ground below, and floated thick around them. He glanced at Bray who was back on his knees digging around in his backpack. When he stood up he wore the goggle-style glasses his stepdad had put in the pack and was fitting a breathing mask to his face. He put it on so fast Zac heard the elastic snap as it was quickly pulled over each ear.

'Ouch,' Bray winced. 'Here, get this on.' He handed goggles and a breathing mask to Zac.

Neither spoke about his stepdad and this second fluke. The correct gear just happened to be packed. It was too weird.

'Better.' Bray lifted his mask and spoke close to his friend's ear before he quickly adjusted the mask back over his mouth. The volcanic ash left a burnt bitter taste on his lips.

Zac nodded. 'Can you hear me?' he said without lifting his mask.

Bray put his thumb up. 'Clearly.'

The boys focused for a minute on the horses. They shook their heads, so their manes moved majestically and then snorted.

'Are they talking to each other?' Zac turned to Bray.

'Guess so. Up here anything's possible. Let's face it, we thought mythology was a myth,' Bray said.

The thunderous noise became louder, and had them look down. A river of red lava had been exposed and ran below them. They knew enough to know this area on Mars was experiencing an earthquake. The gaping crevice continued to open up all the way to the mountain they headed for. Once it hit the mountain, the impact of the crack in the crust caused the mountain to erupt. Molten lava came first, but combined with the earthquake, there was an almighty explosion. The blast sent fire and glowing red hot rocks out into the atmosphere. Bray spun on his heels to get a reading from the NAVscan. In the right position he could see the view panel clearly. He knew from the red dot that headed at a rapid speed away from them that they had a problem.

'The artefact! It's heading towards outer space. We have to follow it.' Bray yelled over the loud groans of land breaking apart and the noise of a river that ran full of boiling liquid.

'Seriously, we won't catch it. That thing looks like it has the power of a rocket. We only have horses,' Zac replied.

Bray could see he wore a frown by the way his dark eyebrows disappeared below the goggles. 'Regardless, that chunk that just broke away has our disc thing in it. We have to go after it,' Bray stressed.

Zac called to the horses. 'Go after that chunk of rock,' and he flicked hard at the reins.

The horses bolted off. The lead horse turned its head and eyed Zac.

Adventures of Bray and Zac

'That bit there!' He pointed.

The horse turned and snorted, steering the others in the direction. At the same time another explosion had boiling plasma, fire and rock spew out towards them. They thought they were safe inside the chariot until a red ember rock smashed into the side of it. The force tossed the boys sideways. It was Bray's quick thinking that saved him and Zac from falling to their death. He looped his backpack around the decorative side panel and held on to it with one hand and Zac with the other.

With a lot of grunting, Zac pulled himself back inside the chariot. He helped Bray, who half hung out, back inside. With the side panel now on fire, Bray scrambled to his feet.

'What the hell happened?' Bray yelled as he unhooked his bag. He was confused as he fumbled inside for the fire extinguisher. 'We are meant to be safe in the chariot. How did it catch on fire? The entire side is up in flames.'

On finding the extinguisher, he flipped off the safety lock, aimed and sprayed. He was surprised at how much liquid foam came out. The contents soon extinguished the flame.

With the fire out he helped Zac to his feet. 'You okay buddy?' He could see he was deep in thought.

'I just had a notion. What if something else is controlling the chariot. Let's face it, Helios was nowhere in sight.' Zac frowned.

'I see where you're going with this. Without his magic it may be quite possible for molten rock to penetrate the chariot.'

'Do you agree that's what is going on here Bray?'

Bray shrugged. 'At this stage I'm not ruling anything out. Even if it is a little far-fetched. What I am sure of, we did need that fire extinguisher. That stepdad of mine is too spooky.'

'That's it Bray, bet he's one of those physics. He thinks he can see into the future. We can just say we never needed any of his gear and he'll think he is wrong about what you are up to and stop it. We know we can't tell anyone.'

'Good point. Put him off the track. I like that!' Bray smiled.

Zac blinked, took a deep breath and, getting up, took the reins. 'Now let's get back on track, get the artefact and go home.'

'Good plan,' said Bray.

Zac turned back to him, worried. 'The horses, Bray!'

They looked out at the horses who were about to be sprayed with the hot rocks that spewed out around them. They were glad when they saw sparks of fire and rocks bounce off a silver glow that appeared, like a shield, around each horse. But before they could relax, one bounced off and headed towards them.

'Ooouch! Cripes that hurts.' Zac screamed out and brushed madly at his arm that was hit by a scalding rock.

'Zac buddy, tie the reins off. I'm coming to help.' Bray called to him. Knowing what he had to do he ripped at the plastic that covered the fire blankets and carefully placed one over Zac who had been hit again, almost in the same spot. 'It's okay Zac, you'll be safe under here.' Next he pulled the other one over his own head. 'We have to huddle together. Don't worry about the horses.' He had seen Zac's concerned look towards them. 'They know where to go.'

Zac's pain became unbearable. He shook and through tears and gritted teeth growled, 'It really hurts Bray. I hate pain!' He grimaced.

Bray had already lifted up the arm of his shirt and was applying the burn cream from the safety pack. 'Better?' He heard his groaning subside and he had stopped panting in pain.

He nodded and took a deep breath. 'Your stepdad is the best. He thinks of everything. That stuff has stopped it burning, fully.' He took a look at the mark and as he did so, the redness dissolved. Not even a scar could they see. 'What is that?'

Bray turned the tube around but the label just said, *burn cream*. 'No idea bud. Another Eishol invention. The guy must be into chemistry as well. Wonder if Mum knows she married the biggest geek ever.'

Zac chuckled. 'She sure does attract them. I mean, you, me, now him.'

They laughed. Their chuckles sounded even funnier through the masks they wore. It was spontaneous hysteria, a nervous reaction, and for a moment allowed the fear of their situation to seem a little less scary. The chariot was not protected as they thought. That was both a shock and the knowledge frightening.

Chapter Ten

Bray had a peek out from under the fire blanket where he hid. 'Look Zac! The artefact is heading for that moon.'

Zac uncovered his head, his fingers rubbing his scalp. 'That blanket makes me itch.' He kept scratching while focusing on the two moons. 'The one it's heading for is called Phobos. If it's going to land on one of those moons, you'd want it to be that one. It's similar to Earth. Deimos on the other hand has very little gravity. Also it gets hit by meteorites so the craters become covered by debris and dust. Finding our artefact would be unlikely. We'd choke to death on the dust if we climbed into one of those holes.'

Cross-legged they both ducked back under their blankets as a rocket-sounding explosion shot past them. They faced each other, keeping the fire blankets together so no hot rocks could slip between them. The pounding felt like hailstones against a tent.

'Phew, think I just shat myself.' Bray put on a brave front to keep Zac calm. His eyes were boggled inside his goggles.

'Bray, this isn't cool. Let's tell the horses to take us home. We have time. We can come back tomorrow night and get it from the moon.'

'I agree. But something's not right. We shouldn't be here at all tonight. But somehow Helios has put thoughts into my stepdad's head to give us this stuff to protect us. We have nothing much else in the kit. I used nearly all of it, so I'm sure this is the end of things that could go wrong.' Bray wasn't sure about much but was sure they were being looked after by the god.

Zac was quiet, his head hung as he pondered that logic. 'I guess so… but I'm still not sure why Helios and Ochimus weren't in sight. Or why there were no horsemen to tend to the steeds. Maybe they're in trouble for helping us.'

'Maybe all this is leading us to them.' Bray's grin showed he was enjoying this mystery, even if it was scary. 'How cool if we're their saviours and… we have to rescue them.'

Zac's eyes widened as did his smile. Helios was the only god willing to save mankind. To return the favour and be able to save Helios, and help him in return was a real buzz for him.

'Pay it forward.' Zac looked up, put his fist in the air and punched the nothingness with gusto. 'I love being the chosen one.'

'Me too!' Bray was sceptical of their theory that a *god* would need saving. But he enjoyed this adventure and even though it was the scariest thing he had ever done, his love of astronomy kept him on course. To go home would be to give up and he had no intentions of doing that. This wasn't about saving the world anymore as much as it was about saving one person, his mum. The minute fear gripped him, he felt her near. Her soft voice egged him on in times of despair and uncertainty. She supported him through any task he tackled. That encouragement warmed him now and dissolved his fear. He had to complete this mission, for her, for them, for the world.

Zac broke through his thoughts. 'To be one day ahead gives us time if anything goes wrong. We are going to be so looking good by day seven.'

Bray nodded in agreement. 'Imagine, we won't have to rush on the last day to retrieve the last piece of the puzzle. We can use that time busting our brain cells getting them to form into the weapon, maybe a missile.'

Adventures of Bray and Zac

Bray turned on the screen of the NAVscan. 'Hey it's stopped. Let's take a peep.' As he thought, the horses had slowed down and he figured they waited for a new command. There was no fire, molten lava or hot rock shards to be seen. In fact they were looking at clear sky and the ground below was icy and very uneven. Bray pulled off his mask and goggles before he tossed off the blanket.

Zac removed his face mask and pulled his goggles up on his head. 'Nice,' he said before he got up and leaned on Bray's shoulder so he could see the NAVscan. 'You were right. It's over, and look at this view.' He let out a whistle. 'Can't believe I nearly forced us to miss this. Phobos is amazing. What's our location? That is one ginormous crater. Bet it's Stickney. It's meant to be ten kilometres in diameter.'

'Nope, not that one. We're too close to the south pole. See the icelands?' Bray pointed to the south of them. He tapped the screen twice which enlarged the area allowing them to view the details. 'It's Hall Crater. The second largest on Phobos. This crater is six km in diameter,' said Bray.

'The artefact has fallen in. Looks like it's gone deep.' Zac pointed to the dot that kept flashing. 'We have no climbing gear. What now boy genius?' He grinned, enjoying the experience now the battlefield had gone. 'Hey what's that other dot flashing?' He saw the new signal the same time as

Bray.

'It's there, just below the ice. We best take a look in case it broke in half or something,' said Bray.

'It looks easy to get at. I'll move the horses closer to it.' Zac undid and picked up the reins. He glanced at Bray. 'Hang on buddy. We better put our jacket on. It looks bitterly cold out there and I'm not sure if we are protected by this chariot any more. Who knows what's going on with it?'

Bray pulled a jacket and a woollen jumper out of his backpack. 'Here, you get colder than me.' He handed Zac the jacket. After wiggling into the thick jumper his mum had knitted him, Bray picked up the NAVscan. 'At least this thing is still working,' he told Zac. 'The temperature is showing minus five degrees at that location. We should be okay in what we have on to make a quick dash to retrieve whatever is beeping.'

Just then something rolled out from the zipped compartments where he'd dug around and found his beanie. Bray picked it up. 'What's this?' He held up the spray can.

'What is it?' Zac turned and squinted to see.

'It's a can of compressed air.' Bray shook it.

'What would we use it for? Leave it here to

save carrying it.' Zac turned back to the horses.

Bray shrugged and placed the items back in his backpack. 'You never know. Best take it.' He slipped the straps over his shoulders and secured the bag on his back, clasping the clips firmly into place. Warm and ready, he waited with gusto, looking forward to the recovery.

Zac was having an entirely different experience. His smiled wide as he flicked the leather and gave the signal for four magnificent steeds to get moving. Chuffed with his new skill of steering the chariot, Zac called to them. 'Pyrios, Aeos, Aethon and Phlegon, we are heading north.' He pulled on the reins, and added, 'quickly now, there's no time to waste.'

Bray chuckled. 'You love driving this chariot a bit too much Zac. Just remember, we have to hand it back at the end of the week.'

Zac called over his shoulder, the wind whizzing past now they had speed up, 'Then I will have to double enjoy my time with these magnificent beasts while I have them.' He gave the reins another shake. 'Pyrios, Aeos, Aethon and Phlegon, faster my new friends.'

The biggest horse, Pyrios, turned its head towards Zac and seemed to grin, before turning back. The chariot shot off so fast the cart shook making the two boys' voices vibrate when they talked, cracking them up in fits of laughter.

Chapter Eleven

The Rescue

Bray and Zac had left the chariot in search of what they figured was the second half of the artefact. Standing above the location Bray dropped to his knees. The ice immediately felt wet but with no other choice except to use his leather-gloved hands, he began to dig away the powdery surface snow. 'It's here. It has to be,' he said as he used his hands as a shovel to remove it. The pile of snow to the left of him grew. Suddenly his hands hit something hard. 'What have we here?' He looked up at Zac.

Zac had only cloth material gloves on. He stood watching with hands in his pockets not wanting to get wet. But this yanked at his curiosity. After removing his gloves he slipped them in his pocket to keep them dry and joined Bray on the ground. 'Is it the box?

'It's grey and has no markings on it,' said

Bray.

Zac helped dig feverishly to uncover the metal square. 'It's a manhole hatch,' he sang out while he held cold fingers together and blew warm air from his mouth into them to warm his fingers. 'But what's it doing way out in the middle of nowhere? I don't get what this has to do with the artefact.' He slipped his gloves back on now the digging had finished.

'Maybe nothing. The signal is most likely being picked up by accident. Could be that it's made from the same material as our artefact.' He eyed Zac. 'Want to take a look?' His eyebrow went up.

'How? We have no key.'

'True, but we do have that can of compressed air. Reach into the zipped pouch on my backpack and hand it to me?' Bray snapped his fingers for it in a hurry while he took a good look at the lock.

Zac shrugged, pulled the can out and handed it to him.

'You wouldn't happen to have a hammer would you?' Bray said.

'No, but I have steel-tipped work boots on.' Zac stood and showed him his boots.

The Magic Portal

'Okay that might work.' Bray started to spray the lock. As he did the lock and hinge started to freeze.

'What! No way.' Zac bent down to watch.

'I heard the science teacher say it's compressed difluoroethane. I guessed this would work.'

'Nice.' Zac nodded.

'Okay, you're up.' Bray got out of the way. 'Give it a good kick.'

Using the toe of his boot, Zac gave the lock a couple of short but sharp kicks and it smashed to pieces. 'Cool, I really should start listening more.' He helped Bray lift the heavy metal lid. 'What's in there?' Zac peered around Bray's head trying to see down the shaft.

Bray moved his head out of the way. He looked up. 'Just a ladder leading down. It's deep. Very deep.'

'We don't need to see what's down there... Do we?' Zac's voice got squeaky as he looked down into the pit below. His fear of heights had well and truly been tested on this journey.

'Hell yes; we're here aren't we? Look, it can't be any worse than the climb up that mountain. Tell me you're not going to let your phobia stop you. It hasn't up until now. This will be easy and who knows… Maybe there is another part to the missile we're to launch in…' He lifted his jacket sleeve to look at his watch. 'In approximately four days and four hours' time.'

'What, we still have four hours left to complete this mission?' Zac put his hands on his hips thinking. 'I figure this will be about half an hour down and back,' he shrugged. 'Guess we still have plenty of time to retrieve the other piece of artefact before we're sent home. Okay I'm in.'

Bray turned around and, getting a foothold on the first rung of the ladder, carefully started his descent. Zac was close behind him.

It got darker as they made their way to the bottom. A slight flicker of light came from the ground, which kept them from climbing into complete blackness. At the bottom Bray breathed out heavily as he jumped onto a metal surface. 'You right, Zac?' He helped his buddy.

'Sure, but there's nothing here. Just a door. And it's locked too.'

Bray pulled the can out of his pocket. 'Not for long.' He sprayed this lock.

'What if something is down here like an alien or a three headed dog, or… *or…* maybe Medusa? We could be turned to stone and goodbye universe!'

Bray chuckled. 'You have such an out there imagination.'

'But seriously,' said Zac, 'doors are generally locked for a reason. Let's leave it and let someone else deal with it.'

'Come on buddy, where's your sense of adventure? Let's take one quick look,' said Bray.

'If you really want to Bray, you know I've got your back. As if I'd let you go on your own.'

'I know, Zac. You're a good friend. And if there are any more locks, we can't go any farther anyway. This can is empty. So how about you use your boot one last time and we'll see where it takes us,' said Bray.

Zac nodded in agreement and slammed his boot down on the lock. The hinged clamp smashed to pieces as the other had.

The door swung open and both boys stood with their mouths open.

'What the—!' Bray blinked, hardly believing his eyes. 'Come on Zac, help me untie them.'

'What's going on?' Zac stared at the several figures, bound and gagged on the floor.

Bray untied the gag and ropes that restrained Helios.

'Drink?' Helios pointed to the bag he carried.

While Bray dug around in his backpack for his drink container, Zac untied his son, Ochimus, and started on the bull men who cared for the horses. 'You guys okay?' said Zac.

The bull men nodded. Their big horns were wrapped in alien cloth.

Bray left Helios to share a drink with Ochimus and moved over the other side of the room to help Zac. 'Gee they thought of everything. No way could they have used their horns to help get free, when they were tied up like this.' Bray shook his head.

'Who would do something like this? And, Yuk! This stuff feels disgusting.' Zac shuddered as he helped to remove the sticky slime-like cloth.

'Got no more water left, bull men.' Then Bray grinned with a thought. 'But there is a crap load of snow out there if you guys want to graze.'

The biggest bull man snorted loudly in his face, unimpressed.

'Hey, don't go rumbling your voice at me, we just saved your butts so don't spray snot on me, you big ringed-nosed bully.' His words were insulting, but he kept his tone friendly, hoping they could take a joke.

The four bull men stood up, towering over him. Without a word they clip-clopped out the door. It was then Bray noticed that even though they had the head of a bull and body of a man, their back legs they walked on were those of a bull, hoofs and all. Yet their hands, although hairy, were human. This didn't excuse the fact they were rude and he called out to them as he heard them begin a noisy climb up the ladder. 'Yep, thanks for saving us?' He called after them. 'No, really, it was my pleasure. Ungrateful sods.'

'Bray, stop it,' Zac hissed. 'Don't they scare you even a bit?'

'Nope.' Bray turned to Helios with his hands on his hips. 'Me and my boy here went through some scary stuff to get here. I want to know what's going on. This experience is way beyond child's play, so fill us in. You never know, we might be the only ones who can help.'

Helios moved his head to the side and eyed them for what seemed ages. Finally he must have decided to give the boys a shot at helping them and spoke. 'Well firstly, the only reason you are still alive after the display with the Bullmasters, not bull men, is because they *are* grateful. You see, they don't talk human language. That's why they did not thank you in your native tongue. That snort you objected to was them saying they appreciate what you did. You were also very helpful as they were thirsty and would now have their thirsts quenched. So even though you were rude to them, they would hold you in high standing for what you have done for them.'

'Oops!' Bray chuckled. 'I got that wrong.'

Helios gave a tired movement that showed his amusement. 'You sure did. Now help me and my son to our feet. We've been down in this ice prison for far too many hours. It has weakened our powers.' His voice faded.

Ochimus spoke for his father. 'All we had was used to practically blow up a planet and get you boys to come here.'

'Couldn't you use that magic to free yourselves,' said Bray.

'The chemcial in these chains does not respond to our magic and was slowly killing us. And the material covering the Bullmasters prevents them from moving. Not sure we would have lasted much longer had you decided to go to the second location on your scanner. Our power was so depleted we couldn't even help with the lock. How you broke it is a miracle. So trust you? Yes, my father wants you to know that you have proved to be very resourceful, brave and trustworthy. But he has to go home to recharge our power.'

Both boys nudged one another, chuffed they were trusted, and beamed a big smile as they went to Helios. They took an arm each and after a lot of grunting by them, got the huge powerful man to his feet.

'You right there big fella?' Bray asked as he steadied Helios.

'My son!' He pointed to Zac, now trying to lug Ochimus to his feet. 'Help him!'

'Oh I see. Now you don't need me it's back to your old-grumpy, pomposity again.' Bray dropped his hand and backed away from him. 'Fine!' he snapped and spun around to help Zac with Ochimus.

Ochimus turned to Zac. 'It's true then.'

Zac blinked, uncertain what he meant.

'I mean about redheads. Your mate's a fiery little one, is he not.'

'Hello, I'm here beside you,' Bray said.

Zac smiled at Bray. 'He is one feisty tiger but you couldn't find a better friend. He practically talked himself hoarse getting me not to turn around and go home. Us being here is all him. That gung-ho attitude is the stuff of heroes on our planet.'

Ochimus was standing now and turned to face Bray. 'Then we owe you our lives young man. Whatever you need, ask.'

Bray thought for a while and his eyes watered. 'My mum. If me and Zac don't make it, if something goes wrong down there, save my mum.' He watched as Ochimus glared at his dad who nodded. He stretched out his arm and Bray took the hand he offered and shook it.

'Done, my new friend. Now get us out of here and fast. My father looks unwell.'

Bray lifted the hand he held up and over his shoulder to help support Ochimus as they walked.

'Zac, you're taller and stronger than me, so help Helios to the ladder. We don't have much time if I've read this right. If we are being tracked, we have to get these two to the chariot and fast.'

'Maybe we better think about a plan B, Bray.' Zac spoke as he helped Helios.

'Hiding them you mean?'

'Well they would be crazy to go home. It will be straight back here or somewhere similar.' Zac grunted as Helios stumbled and he held him upright.

'Agree. Whoever did this wanted them dead. Any bets the kidnappers' plan was to sabotage our mission?'

Bray had already got Ochimus to the ladder. Zac came up behind them and leant Helios against the wall next to it.

'Smart boys,' Helios replied quietly. His poor health made Bray feel bad he snapped at the ancient dude. He turned. 'You were just worried for your son. I was rude.'

'Yes.' The god's reply was barely a whisper.

Once Ochimus had hold of the ladder, Bray shifted to the left of it to allow Helios access. 'You're next Helios!'

The god gave him a slight smile before he reefed his heavy body up the first rung with a groan.

'Come on old dude, you got more in you than that. You gunna let your son show you up.' Bray gave encouragement.

'Cheeky sod!' Bray heard Helios groan out. The overly large man swore many times as he dragged his weary body up one rung at a time.

When Ochimus reached the top Bray yelled

out, 'We parked in an ice cave to the left.'

At the top the son was helping his dad to the cave that was easily visible from the ground. When Bray and Zac arrived at the cave, they watched the Bullmasters use the last of their magic to enlarge the chariot. Now they would all fit.

'Zac you drive the horses, I'll get the others comfortable.'

'Where am I taking us?'

'Until I'm able to help, just tell the horses to get us away from here. Straight ahead will do. We can come back tomorrow and grab the artefact.'

'No!' They heard a squeak from Ochimus. 'Father said you must get it now. He doesn't want you coming back here.'

With a flick of the reins they were on their way. While Zac drove, Bray covered the passengers with the fire blankets to keep them warm, before joining Zac up the front. 'It's to the left a little.' Bray pointed.

'How lucky is that. It landed on that ledge. The shelf is just the right size. I'll be able to land the chariot and horses on it. If you jump out and grab it, we are out of here in minutes.' Zac peered over his shoulder. 'They okay?'

'The son is in better shape than the others after having the water I gave him. He said he will look after Helios. And that the Bullmasters just need to warm up and they will be fine.'

Zac smiled. 'Well they are immortal. Live forever and all that. Not sure if a bit of cold would do much damage.'

Bray agreed. 'I bet because they never get sick, a little cold makes for a drama hey.'

They both chuckled at that thought as Zac guided the chariot down. The horses had to adjust to the heavy load they carried and skidded more than Zac anticipated. The edge came near as the four horses dug into the snow-covered shelf, skidding so close to the edge Zac was ready to fly them off it. But at the last second their hooves gripped and they came to a sudden halt.

With both hands on the edge of the chariot, Bray lifted quickly over the side and sprinted to the artefact. Using the camera on the NAVscan he took a photo of the marking on the box before opening it. The disc slid from it easily and before running off he placed it in his pocket. Something made him look up, but the ledge they were on was tucked inside the wall of the crater, so he could see nothing. However, it made him nervous that the kidnappers, whoever they were, could be looking for Helios and his son already. He raced back to the chariot and was puffing hard as he jumped aboard.

'I thought I saw a shadow over me. Did you guys see anything?'

'Nothing,' Zac said, slightly alarmed. 'Should we wait a bit?'

From the back of the chariot, Helios said, 'My horses can outrun anything. Go now!'

'You heard the man,' Bray patted at his chest to calm down.

Zac called out, 'Pyrios, Aeos, Aethon and Phlegon. As fast as you can take us from here.' He turned to the others. 'We can hide you at my place if it is too dangerous up here. Our house backs onto a property we also own. No one is renting it. I can get the key.'

'Good idea Zac. I was thinking about my place but it's far too small. Bray turned to Helios. 'The rental is on a large block with a big barn. The horses can rest and stay out of view. You and your son and the Bullmasters can do the same. It's summer where we live and stinking hot. At least come and get warm.'

Helios nodded. 'Fly the horses directly to Earth. I have no magic to use the portal.' Wearily he put his head back down.

'Are you sure Father?' Bray heard Ochimus ask.

'Yes!' was the firm reply.

Chapter Twelve

The Hideout

After hiding the chariot, Pyrios, Aeos, Aethon and Phlegon in the barn, they left the Bullmasters to attend to the horses. After a sleep on the way down to Earth the Bullmasters changed from a shade of ice blue back to the dark-skinned horned men they usually were. Zac and Bray retrieved the key from Zac's house.

The rental was partly furnished so they had only to bring back bedding and food. In Zac's freezer they found soup which they heated. His sister had filled the bread maker and the loaf had only just finished its baking cycle.

'Bring the fresh loaf with us, Bray. My sister will think I ate it and make more when she gets up. She's used to me having a midnight snack,' Zac said.

'I think she bakes it for you especially Zac.

Contrary to her snide remarks I think she really does care about you.'

Zac smiled. 'Never thought about it like that. She has never gone crook at me eating it.'

'What about this apple pie?' Bray had his head in the fridge.

'Sure, we can take that too. Only just pulled it out the freezer for a snack last night. That was before we were swallowed up in the book.' He chuckled and took a tub of ice cream from the freezer to go with it. He picked up the bowl of fruit and shook it into the bag where he and Bray had put the food and items to take to the gods.

'That should do them.' Bray grabbed one of the handles and Zac the other.

When they got back they opened up the house and let Helios and Ochimus inside. The food they placed out on the table as a banquet. 'Even though it's hot, we packed in the bag a couple of throw rugs and some sheets and pillows for the bed,' Zac said as they finished adding the last bits of fruit to the display. 'Hope there's enough here. Will bring more in the morning.'

Helios was pacing, then yelled at the Bullmasters.

Ochimus shrugged. 'Thanks boys. That will

be fine. Go get some sleep.'

'You don't have to tell us twice.' Bray rubbed his eyes. 'Ready Zac?'

'Sure am,' he agreed.

Tired, they left their guests to enjoy the feast they felt proud of putting together.

'Helios will feel better once he eats.' Bray nudged Zac. Good job buddy.'

'Thanks for helping Bray. We did good tonight didn't we?' Zac grinned.

'Real good,' said Bray.

Both went their separate ways once they got to the gate. Bray ran the rest of the way home.

At home Bray hid the disc he had retrieved and flopped on the bed. It was after midnight and yet Bray was finding it hard to sleep. He tossed and turned restlessly, sitting up when the door opened. It was his mum.

'Are you okay Mum?' He could see tears on her cheeks from the moonlight that shone bright through his window.

'Thank God you're home and okay!' She strode over, dropped heavily beside him and hugged him tight.

'Mum, I was with Zac. I thought Eishol was taking you to dinner! He bought ours for us. We... we were out stargazing and forgot the time. I didn't mean to scare you.' He kept talking to calm her.

'Eishol didn't come home.' She shook her head.

'Really?' He pulled out of the hug to see her face. His mind was going faster by the second as he recalled the last moments he saw Eishol.

Helios had been kidnapped about the same time as Eishol's disappearance.

Eishol... Helios... same letters... He'd always thought *Eishol* was a weird name.

He stared and gulped. 'Mum do you trust how much I love you?'

'Of course I do! But what has this to do with anything?' she said.

'Mum, you have to trust me as much as you love me.'

'I do sweetheart, but what's all this about?' She lifted his chin, searching his face.

'I can explain on the way. Go pack an overnight bag and meet me at the front door. I have to show you something and I think if I'm right, you are going to be really happy. I hope so... but it means we have to leave here immediately.'

She breathed out. 'Okay Bray. I guessed you and Eishol were up to something because you have started to get on...' Her hands were on her hips.

'Mum, please. We have to leave immediately,' he said.

'I guess it's time I gave you the trust you have always given me Bray. I'll grab my bag and meet you in a tick at the front door. Okay?'

After what happened to Helios and his son. Bray freaked out, at who may be at the front door. 'No! Back door.'

'Back door then.' She smiled the way she did when he was doing something that made her happy, like washing dishes and cleaning up after himself.

'Love you Mum.' He smiled back.

As soon as she left the room he picked up the two-way. 'Zac, you there buddy?' he called to him as he took the old CD player off the shelf where the discs were hidden. Quickly he tipped out the contents of his backpack and slid out the hard bottom, where his mum had sewn in a secret compartment for his personal bits and pieces.

This had happened after he'd confided he

was being bullied for lunch money at school. She had got right to work with a needle and thread. 'They can shake this bag empty now sweetheart,' she told him smiling. 'And this compartment will never come out.'

He smiled, remembering how glad he was of her handiwork the very next day.

Confident this was the best place to keep them, he slipped the discs inside and re-applied the straps and false bottom.

'What's up? Can't sleep either?' Zac's voice came over the two-way.

'Hey, we have a situation. Can you check if anyone suspicious is lurking around outside?' Bray started filling the backpack with gear he thought he might need.

'Hells bells what's going on?' Zac peeped outside. 'Can't see anyone.'

Bray leaned over and picked up the two-way. 'Do you know Eishol didn't come home? He disappeared after dropping us off and that was about the same time Helios was kidnapped.'

'Geez then someone might be after us?' Zac squeaked out.

'Exactly, so I'm leaving now with Mum.

Meet us out the back of your house. I think you know what I'm thinking. We better not talk over this thing. Talk when I see you.'

Bray raced downstairs. He only waited a few seconds before his mum joined him. He hushed her. 'Quiet,' he whispered.

She nodded and followed.

They quickly moved around the back of the house and through the neighbour's gate.

Once back out on the road, Bray confidently walked across the road with his mum, even holding her arm so they looked as if they were just heading home after a nice dinner party. Fortunately all their neighbours had put in a gate for access when the boys were younger, so it wasn't long before Bray and his mum were walking into Zac's back yard.

'Now tell me what's going on.' Zac stood holding the treasured library book, his pack slung over one shoulder. 'The big guy will be furious if we turn up with your mum.'

'Think about the names of two weird men,' Bray hinted.

Zac slapped his palm against his forehead. 'No... surely not.'

'His concern for saving us, knowing exactly

what to pack for us... need I say more?' Bray nodded, pinched his lips and lifted his eyebrows.

'Now I get what you meant about them both disappearing at the same time.' Zac shook his head with surprise. 'You're worried if they can't get him to stop they will come after us. And in that case your mum is not safe either.'

'What have you boys got us involved in!' Bray's mum's eyes were wide in disbelief as she broke into the conversation. 'Has Eishol got you boys into something... something...' She was having trouble with the words.

'No Mum! Don't even think that. Eishol would never do anything illegal, but if this person is not Eishol, he is the only person I know who can find him for you.'

'Mrs B, we have much to tell you,' Zac said. 'But you have to wait until we get behind safe closed doors. If what Bray is telling me is true, we have to change our plans... tonight.'

Chapter Thirteen

What's the Plan?

'The lights are still on.' Zac whispered as they moved to the front of the spare house.

The porch squeaked as they stepped onto it and the door flung open. Helios stood ready for battle, his son right behind him.

'Boys, what are you doing here and why did you get your mother involved Bray?' Helios looked cross, but no more than he was when they left him earlier.

'Guess you didn't think about us, did you.' Bray stood up to him. 'If they find you gone and you can't be found, who are they are going to kidnap next to prevent us doing our job... us!'

Helios rubbed his head. 'They wouldn't dare,' he bellowed.

'The kid's got a point, Father,' said Ochimus.

Bray studied Helios, looking at the size of him, considering what he may look like without all that hair. It was hard to imagine the man he hated might actually be the man he admired. He had all but given up when Helios changed his stance. This was a habit Eishol had, whenever Bray stumped him and he didn't know what to say. It was him. Bray also knew Helios could read his mind and right this moment knew his cover was blown.

'We have much to discuss Eishol.' Bray put it out there before he could deny it. He turned to his mother. 'Mum this is the god Helios and his son Ochimus. You know him as Eishol and he is your husband.' He took firm hold of his mum's hand and dragged her inside. There was no resistance. Bray's introduction had surprised her. 'We can talk inside, Mum. The neighbours may hear and this has to stay secret.'

She nodded, her head turned, not taking her eyes off Helios.

Zac followed in last. He closed, locked and bolted the security door and the main door, glad his parents had chosen to buy this rental. The previous owners were very safety conscious.

'I must be dreaming.' Mum stared at Bray, not blinking.

'Most of this will be hard to swallow, Mum,

but the alternative is to watch you grieve and worry yourself sick...' He swallowed, hiding his nervousness, and hoped this was the right decision. *She didn't look that well.* He felt a certain amount of guilt. Not only had she worried when her husband never came, but Bray had not come home until late either. 'Having you sad is worse than having you mad when you find out the truth.'

He hoped if Helios really was Eishol he'd sort this out. Bray had no intentions of leaving his mum sitting at home crying over him.

As soon as the door shut, Helios stood in front of Bray's mum. 'Sorry my love. I wanted to tell you but I couldn't risk you hating me and not allowing me to be there for your son.' He turned magically into Eishol to show her. She gasped and lifted her hand to her mouth. 'It is you?'

'Yes, Madeline, my beautiful wife. It is me, Eishol, but also me Helios, the sun god.'

'A sun god. So you used me to get to my son?' She looked as if she was going to faint. Her face was pale, eyes wide.

'I will not lie to you any more. In the beginning I chose to befriend you to help Bray and Zac fulfil their destinies. I know this will come as a shock, but those two boys are the chosen ones, selected out of all the children on Earth.'

She turned her attention to Bray. 'Bray—'

Bray held up his hand. 'Just hear him out Mum, please!'

Helios waited for Madeline to turn back to him before he continued. 'But the moment we met, your smile stole my heart and your eyes stole my soul.' Worry lines appeared on his forehead. He obviously felt bad about not being there when she got home. He had made her cry. 'I didn't mean to hurt you. But after I dropped the boys off I was kidnapped in the driveway of your home.'

'Kidnapped...' Madeline looked horrified. 'Are you all right?' Being mad at him dissolved into concern.

'Yes, kidnapped, Mum. He didn't mean to make you worry like that.' Bray couldn't work out if he was protecting Helios or Eishol. Did he want his mum happy? *Yes.*

'Thanks Bray, but your mother needs to hear it all. If she is going to be a part of my future, which I want her to be, we must have no more secrets as a family.' Eishol ran a hand through his hair, shaking slightly. Bray could see how upset he was at the thought of losing her. He understood why Helios had been moody. If he loved his mum as he said, he must have felt horrid. Bray knew *he* would, and did, when he wasn't home when she needed him.

But Helios was right, this was between them and funnily enough he really wanted them to sort it out. His stepdad had become likable. Being weird seemed more acceptable, once he thought of him as a sun god. Bray looked up to him, and wished to get to know him more as Eishol. He gestured towards Zac to sit with him at the table. Ochimus followed them and together they sat quietly allowing the two some space.

'What's this about being kidnapped and the chosen ones, Eishol? Is my son in danger too? I don't like what I'm hearing.' His mum talked sternly.

'I will not lie. Yes, he is in danger, but because of his pure heart and compassion.' He stopped and smiled. 'That's something you've given to him. Bray will continue to move mountains to accomplish this mission. I should have known once I met the mother of this young genius, she would blow my mind and I'd be lost to her.'

She glanced over at Bray and smiled, her eyes alight with such a compliment. 'What about Zac? He is from such a different life,' she said.

'His friend Zac was chosen because they complement each other perfectly. Neither will allow the other to fail. This protective friendship has developed over the years and will continue well past this day if they can win against those who oppose this.'

'Oppose this and oppose who? You are talking in riddles,' said Madeline.

'If you permit me to change back to Helios I can show you. The human body masks some of my powers.'

'Sure. But I'm going to need a bit more than smoke and mirrors to convince me. You're asking me to allow my own son to put himself in the arms of danger. I can't even imagine how much it would take to save this world.'

'Save the universe.' Eishol corrected her before he faded and Helios shimmered into focus. Just as he had done for the boys, he showed Madeline what was about to happen. Bray wasn't surprised at her reaction. Tears ran down her face as the planets were one by one destroyed. Her hand shook as it wiped away tears that ran down her face. She blew her nose on the handkerchief Helios handed to her. After she calmed, he showed her the mammoth tasks Bray and Zac already had accomplished when retrieving the artefacts. The boys fist punched as Helios showed the hardest retrieval; the one when they climbed the mountain while on Venus. They felt proud but were blown away Helios had watched and recorded it somehow.

'How did he see all that?' Bray asked Ochimus.

'Helios is the sun god. My father is the only god that can see the past or into the future.'

Helios clapped his hands firmly together, which caused the image to disappear in a smoked effect. Bray wanted to clap as it was so impressive.

'So now you know,' Helios said.

Madeline had her mouth open, still processing what she saw. She tapped her chin, while she regained her thoughts and composure. 'But this is not to happen for many lifetimes yet.'

'That was your son's comment to dismiss reality. But I assure you that it is happening and the boys have five more days to finish collecting four more artefacts from each planet. Once they have all the eight pieces from the eight planets, they have to work out how to build the mechanism. Not only that, they have to work out how to set it off and have it hit right at the beginning of the rip. It has to go through, seal its own tear and when on the other side, suck up the build-up of blackness that threatens our universe.'

'Let's say the weapon doesn't hit its mark. They could go through all this for no reason as it may not even work? This seems a waste of time and all you have are two twelve-year-olds. That's the best you gods can do?'

'The best I can do. You see the other gods

are trying to prevent me and the lads here from succeeding. And please, do not underestimate these two lads. They have already shown me their astute awareness for this mission. I would want no other to finish what they have begun.'

'The others had you kidnapped.' Madeline was shocked.

'Yes! I am lucky you have a bright son with the guts to push past what gets in his way. Between his persistence and Zac's expert handling of my horses that pull the chariot, they saved our lives tonight.' He clasped his hands together and letting them go, opened up his arm wide. This brought up another image, this time showing her Zac being burned and Bray calmly putting cream on him, giving encouragement. The rescue played out and showed how not once did either of them give up.

The teamwork and bravery of her son had Madeline sniffle back into a tissue. She went over and, kneeling in between them, hugged and kissed both boys on the forehead. 'You brave young men. My heart goes out to you both. Are you sure this is real. Am I dreaming?'

Bray hugged her and pulled back to talk. 'Mum it's real. I thought at first I was dreaming too. And I know tomorrow when you wake you will worry for me, but I promise I will be there to have breakfast with you. Zac and I have got this.'

Madeline smiled. 'I believe you have. You sound so much like you father. He would be so proud of you sweetheart.'

'My new father is proud of me too.' He gave Helios a cheeky grin.'

His mum laughed. 'So now I'm ticked off with him, you like him.' Madeline stood and walked back over to Helios. 'You have stolen my son, so I guess we have to work this out.'

'All I can ask is for your forgiveness and understanding. Can you forgive me for lying to you?'

Eyeing Helios she raised an eyebrow. 'You, I do not know yet, but my son seems to believe in you. We will have to start all over again, and I want the whole dating thing this time. Dinner, flowers, chocolates, and being spoilt rotten. If you think you can do this for me, I guess I'll think about forgiving you.'

'I would love to take time to do just that. You are my goddess and so you should be made to feel like one.' He took her hand and kissed it. 'My love, my life, I thank you for this second chance.'

Madeline chuckled at his attention.

While Helios spoke to his Mum, Bray and Zac went into the kitchen to discuss a new plan.

When they came out Helios was still charming his mother and she was falling for him again.

Bray tut-tutted her. 'Come on Mum, make him work harder than that.'

'Shush lad.' Helios smiled at Bray. 'I won her in a weekend. I am as determined as you to make her happy.'

'Touché!' Bray grinned. 'Now if you guys have finished making us ill from all that lovey dovey stuff, can we get down to business?'

'Bray!' his mum disciplined him. 'That is very rude to speak to your elders like that.'

Helios didn't let Madeline's hand go but led her to the table and pulled out a chair for her to sit next to him. 'Although I agree my love, he is right. There is much to discuss. Ochimus and I have come up blank as to where we should go from here. We do not want the lads hurt so are both very interested in what they think.'

'Sorry Mum. I'll try to be more tactful.' Bray answered.

Madeline smiled, pleased for once he actually apologised which was something he never did in front of others.

'Okay lads, floor's all yours,' said Helios.

'Well we were talking about it in the kitchen and we think we have come up with something that might work.' Bray stated.

Zac butted in, 'I agree with Bray. If they couldn't stop you guys helping us then it would be us next.'

'Or maybe Mum as hostage to stop us.' Bray looked worried.

Zac continued. 'So we were thinking, maybe they haven't discovered you've escaped. So we might have another day to complete our mission before it is uncovered that you two are missing from the cave. And regardless of our mission, one of you needs to ride the chariot to drag the sun across the sky.'

'Yes, that is true. The opposers haven't the power to stop the sun coming up. But yes, I will have to do this,' Helios said.

'We guessed that.' Bray glanced at his son and back to Helios. 'But we suggest Ochimus does it as we need you here for our plan to work,' Bray said.

'Why? What plan?' Ochimus leaned forward, unsure where this was going.

'Okay,' Bray smiled. He had their attention. 'What we were thinking is to shake things up.

Change the plan that you originally put in place. Confuse the ones who are trying to stop our quest to save the universe.'

'Go on,' Helios said when Bray stopped to take a drink of water.

He gulped it down and sat the bottle on the table. 'At daybreak while, Ochimus uses the chariot to drag the sun across the sky, we figure we'd use this time as a decoy. Your kidnappers will not think for one minute about us. They will be planning how to stop us when we do arrive on the chariot that night. So we have time to complete our final mission. But not in four days.... in just twelve hours.'

'Without the chariot to get to your planets, how can this happen?' asked Ochimus, looking at Bray as if he had gone quite mad.

'With this book,' said Zac. He held it up with pride that they had come up with what they thought was a great idea. 'What the kidnappers don't know is that there is a portal inside this book. Or at least, we don't think they know.'

Bray grinned. 'Zac's right. So for our plan to work, Ochimus must drive the chariot. Helios will need to stay here guarding this book with Mum, using his magic to send us to the next four planets.'

'Is that right,' Helios scoffed. 'I would

sacrifice my son and hide here. I don't think so!'

'Hang on Father, let's hear him out,' said Ochimus.

Bray continued. 'As I was saying, while Ochimus is in the chariot, nobody will worry about us. They will not be looking to apprehend us until nightfall. However, by then, we will be back here with the last four artefacts.'

'And your plan is for me to send you through the portal in the book,' said Helios.

Bray nodded. 'Just as you use your magic to get us to your chariot.'

Zac chimed in, 'For the first planet only. After that you will need to shift us from planet to planet by looking through the book portal. I am positive this can be done. Am I right?'

Helios rubbed his head. 'In theory it could be done.'

'Okay then,' said Bray. 'If you can send us to the locations where we will find the artefact, we can take it from there. And to make this work, we'll have to collect all four artefacts in twelve Earth hours. This means we will have approximately three hours on each planet ... give or take.'

Zac put the book down on the table. 'If we

leave when the sun comes up, and are home here by the time the sun goes down, then lie low for the next few days, we reckon the ones who oppose us will assume we gave up as we never showed for any further missions. They'll think we never completed what we started.'

Bray continued where Zac left off. 'Once Ochimus lands the chariot we must have completed collecting all four artefacts. Regardless of whether we have or haven't, Helios must bring us back here to safety.'

'Although in saying that, Bray and I believe we can do it in the three hours if we are put closer to the artefacts. Sometimes it made it hard finding somewhere to land the chariot,' Zac grinned.

'True,' Bray agreed. 'Afterwards, it's a simple matter of us lying low as we said, for the next few days. This free time we can use to study. Work out how to get the missile or whatever it is, to form and go do what it's meant to do.'

Helios turned to Ochimus. 'It could just work son. But your safety still concerns me. What are your thoughts?'

Ochimus sat back considering. 'I think it might just work. But...' He put his hand up for quiet. 'If my father can send you to different planets using that book, I can see no reason why we could not use it to bring me back here after my shift. Is this workable Father?'

'Yes son. And you have just won me over. Quite happy to stay here now I know you will be safe. As soon as you land the chariot at the palace, I will not only have you out of harm's way, but will send the Bullmasters through to tend to my horses.' He wore a smile. 'Very pleased with this so far. I like it!' Helios thumped his hand on the desk. 'Bravo... now let's fine-tune this. We have little time before daylight.'

Chapter Fourteen

The Plan

'Bray opened up his backpack. He pulled out the NAVscan and placed it in front of him then removed pens and notepad, handing them to Helios. 'Figure you may not be up to our technology.'

'Cheeky sod. Who sent you that NAVscan?' Helios chastised.

'Probably Ochimus.' He chuckled.

His son laughed, which made Helios laugh. 'Okay, you got me. You kids today put my old ways to shame.'

'Never.' Bray's mum smiled at him. 'I love your old ways.'

'Thank you honey!' He patted her hand that he now held.

'Come on guys. You're making us want to

throw up,' Bray grumbled.

They all had a good laugh, which relieved much of the tension, before they got down to business. From where they sat, Zac had already connected up to the Wi-Fi in his own home and had the satellite working on his laptop. He worked hard, ignoring the bantering going on around the table. He didn't have a happy family environment and Bray could see he was extremely uncomfortable.

'Hey Zac, tell them what Grogan did to us the other day at school.'

Zac started to tell them and as the story continued with them standing in their underpants and their clothes hanging in the tree. The laughter was so loud he exaggerated the truth, just a little. He finally found out how much fun it can be to tell an embarrassing story to the ones who love and care about you.

After the laughter died down it was time to get down to work. Bray and Zac had to pinpoint the landing location on each planet, first choosing an area closest to the artefact, but then finding where best Helios could safely land them. They both knew the book would not change and they'd be tossed roughly through the portal. This needed some thought and had to be precise.

'It's time up.' The sound of Helios's godly

booming voice stopped them. 'It's time for my son to leave. And you lads have to begin your planetary expedition.'

'But we haven't finished!' Bray looked up, stressed. 'Just a couple more minutes. Neptune is our last planet and we haven't finalised our landing coordinates yet. We need to finish this.'

'Your journey begins now and no arguments. Suit up lads.' Helios used his magic to conjure two special suits, gloves, full helmets and strange boots with a fifteen centimetre heel. 'Quickly now,' he rushed them. 'Just remember you will feel heavier up there due to the gravity being greater than here. Times your weight by 2.4 and that's how much heavier you will feel.'

Zac was concerned. 'This is too rushed. Maybe we should wait another day to plan it better. I mean Jupiter, Saturn, Uranus and Neptune are large giant gas planets. Their atmospheres are basically all hydrogen and helium or other gases. Landing on a surface that is made up of so much gas would be stupid. We would be sucked down deep into the molten core.'

Bray agreed. 'Take Jupiter for example. Earth could fit inside it 1000 times and it's a very stormy planet. We could be lost in gas and storm current and never hit the crust. We have given you our landing coordinates but what happens once we land there, hasn't been discussed.'

'Like, how will we breathe without the chariot protecting us?' Zac added.

'Leave those details to me. You will find I am not so old school as you think,' said Helios. 'Now get geared up. Time to go.'

Both did as he commanded. Bray and Zac zipped up their suits and started to put on gloves.

'Hang on, this beeping thing has moved,' Bray's mum chimed in as she kept a watchful eye on the screen.

Bray moved over to the table and picked up the NAVscan. 'It knows we're coming, Zac. It's airborne and moving around the outer ring of gas.'

Zac turned to stare at Helios. 'Okay cross out the crust landing. To pick it up now, the only way is to be airborne. How do we fly?'

'And if we could fly we still have two problems. Firstly Jupiter has winds of 192 to 400 miles per hour so how do you fly in that? Secondly, the atmosphere is full of clouds that are like an ocean filled with liquid metallic hydrogen. I mean, it's not only the gale force winds we would struggle with, but the magnetic force field up there is twenty times stronger than here on Earth. I'm with Zac on this one. We thought we could do it without the chariot.

But after studying these gas globes, I can't see how this is going to work. You should have warned us what an impossible task these gas planets would be without your magical horse-driven ride.'

Bray held Helios's gaze. They needed more than these magical outfits. This was the first time he had agreed with Zac. They had been rash and were jumping in to this unprepared.

'Ye of little faith.' Helios smiled. 'Those shoes you now wear have alien technology. Tap the heels together and you get three hours' burn time, just enough to keep you from falling. So I hope you learn to use them quickly.' He chuckled. 'Oh, I'm going to love watching this rescue.'

Bray twisted his mouth up. 'Good one. Give us a new toy to play with and they're useless when we get home. So, genius, how do we breathe?'

'Through those full head helmets you have just put on. That spacesuit and helmet I created will give you twelve hours of comfortable protection from the elements.'

'After that?' Bray said.

'You better be here!' Helios warned.

Ochimus stood with his hands on his hips listening and shook his head. 'You mortals are so unequipped for life in this universe. Maybe we should let you perish. Are you sure they are worth it, Father?' He wore a smile.

'You...' Helios screwed up his lips, holding back laughter. 'You get to the chariot. I'll use my power to create a vision bubble to watch for you at sundown. That way I can remove you before those who oppose us can get their hands on you.'

'Thank you, Father,' said Ochimus, inclining his head to show his respect. But he couldn't help but speak out. Even though he had become attached to the boys too, he had never had to compete for his father's accolades. This was new having to share him. 'However, I still think you are wasting your energy here. These two whingers will not complete this task without the chariot. When they arrive home without anything tonight... it will be your number one, golden boy that will come up with a suitable plan to fix this.'

Helios grinned. 'Number one pain... now be gone or my plan will be my foot where the sun don't shine.'

Ochimus laughed all the way out the door.

Bray chuckled. 'He means his foot in his arse,' he whispered to Zac. Both found it funny how the god talked sometimes.

Bray might have joked at what was said, but he did enjoy how Helios and his son interacted. He

The Magic Portal

could see how much fun it was going to be to have Helios as his stepdad and didn't mind that thought at all.

'Now, no more stalling. You have studied Jupiter, Saturn and Uranus.'

Both boys laughed when he mentioned Uranus.

'Come on lads, I told you before the joke is getting old,' Helios said.

'Hey we are twelve years old and we're telling you. YOURANUS is very funny.' Bray and Zac cracked up.

'Okay, I get it, now concentrate.' Helios spoke loudly and quietened both boys down. 'Let's look at what we do know so far. You have gone over the first three planets' pick-up points with a fine-tooth comb. You have what you need for this first drop, which is Jupiter. I will make sure you have what is needed as I move you from planet to planet. When you have the artefact, signal me by pressing that red button on the NAVscan. I can move you on to the next planet. After the last planet, which is Neptune, I'll bring you home here.'

Bray held up the NAVscan and flipped a clear window up. 'Wondered what that was for...' He stared at Helios. 'Hang on, what do you mean, Neptune. We haven't even looked at it yet.'

'You will have to trust your mother and me with Neptune. Leave it up to us. We'll research it and work something out. You are your mother's son Bray. And I see from how she has helped with compiling this information today with you, that she is more than competent to help me do the rest.'

'Sure Mum?' Lines appeared on Bray's forehead.

'Trust me sweetheart. Eishol... I mean Helios and I know what you need. I have watched you boys like a hawk.'

'Like a typical mum.' His frown turned to a smile. 'I trust you Mum. Good luck then.' He put a hand on her shoulder. 'And no stressing. Zac and I have dreamed of going on space adventures all our lives. We've got this.'

'I know sweetheart.' She smiled and tapped her cheek. 'Kiss!'

'Mum... do I have to?'

'No, just kidding.' She chuckled. 'Now hop it you two. I need quiet if you want me to get this right for you. I've taken the coordinates from your NAVscan so the rest is just research. Bray, don't worry son... I got this! Okay.'

Bray chuckled at her taking him off. He was so proud of how well she was handling this new life he'd thrown her into and so he kissed her cheek anyway. 'Love you Mum.'

He saw her grin widen. Happy that she was too, he left her side to make a start on the adventure of a lifetime.

'Ready lads? You have three hours on each planet to seek and retrieve the artifacts. At the twelve hour mark it is over. You are coming home ready or not. Understood?'

'It may be down to the wire so it is you who had better not let us down.' Bray gave Helios a bit of attitude.

'Giving the man with the power, cheek. That's gutsy son.' Helios flicked his hands towards them, and both snatched up their bags as they felt themselves being sucked up into the vortex of the book.

'That's why you chose me!' Bray yelled out over the noise as he and Zac disappeared out of sight. Their screams still rang in the air like kids going on those crazy rides at the theme parks.

Bray's mum called out, 'Don't come back dead or I swear I'll be so angry at you.'

Chapter Fifteen

Jupiter

With their arms wrapped around bent legs the boys tumbled into the atmosphere of Jupiter.

'You heard Helios. We have to press our heels together to get them working Zac.' Bray was beside him.

They stretched out their legs and tapped the heels of the boots. With a sudden jolt they stopped and the power of the boots stood them upright. Both boys laughed aloud and punched the air. This set them off balance and they ended up upside down. They both laughed.

'Try punching the air again Bray. Should set us right.'

They both punched at the air and the motion had them standing back up the right way.

'Now to fly.' Bray put his arms out. Nothing

happened. 'What?' He screwed his up face and tried to think flying to see if it worked. He also closed his eyes and imagined he was flying. But nothing happened. He didn't move an inch.

Zac lifted a foot and took a step. 'This works Bray.' He took another step and another.

'Great!' Bray put his hands on his hips. 'Helios did this deliberately. He's going to make us walk... grrr...' He pulled the NAVscan out of his pocket. 'Zac,' he called out. 'This way buddy.' He turned and began walking the opposite way. He waited for Zac to come back to him before stepping alongside him. 'Can we run?'

'I'll try.' Zac made a weird noise as he forced one leg in front of the other. He didn't move any quicker than Bray.

'The artefact is moving away from us, Zac. At this rate it will take us forever to catch it. Stupid boots.'

'Come on. Helios wouldn't have this restriction unless it was necessary. Let's keep experimenting. Something has to work,' said Zac.

Nothing seemed likely.

At last, Bray turned to Zac. 'It's been two hours and forty-five minutes and we are no closer to that artefact. If we don't catch up to it in the next

The Magic Portal

fifteen minutes we'll be pulled off this planet and on to the next by Helios. Remember it was our call and we both said three hours on each planet unless we got to it quicker. Then I'd contact him by pressing the red button on the NAVscan.'

'Then why are we chasing this thing that we can't move quick enough to catch?' said Zac and stopped suddenly. 'May as well leave here and save our energy for the next planet. Not only that, it's still daylight on Earth for hours yet. Here the light is failing and the night is almost upon us.'

Bray stopped too. 'Saturn can wait a few more minutes. We aren't thinking this out logically. We're so busy trying to run or fly to catch our alien piece of equipment, we have missed something that could help us. Okay, so let's think back to what we read about Jupiter. What has that thing moving faster than us? We have gone over every magnetic and analytical atmospheric reason known to man and drawn a blank.'

Zac's eyes stared outward as he cast his memory back. 'Okay, Jupiter's day is ten hours long. So a year on Jupiter is equal to twelve years on Earth. Oh and it spins faster than any other planet.'

'So that explains why it's getting dark. Halve that to ten hours for daylight and the other for the night, give or take. What else does that photographic memory of yours remember, Zac?'

'We are two and a half times our weight up here.' Zac breathed out deeply. 'And I'm feeling every gram.'

'Okay, so we are like lumps of lard trying to catch a determined tortoise.' Bray smiled. 'And as we know, the only way to catch a tortoise is to be smarter.'

Zac lifted his eyebrows in thought. 'Crawl, fly, run, jump. Hey! We haven't tried to jump yet.' His smile was wide.

'There you go, now that's using your noggin. Give it a go brains.'

'I will.' Zac was always ready to back up his ideas. He knew Bray didn't want to end up hanging upside down again. 'So trial one…' He made a noise as if he was turning on his two way. Zac liked it when he made his friend smile.

'Try taking some steps first Zac. Then jump.'

Zac nodded. The first three were steps to get momentum then using his body he lifted in an upward motion. The first jump was small, but with every jump he got farther each time.

Getting away from him, Bray copied him. Again the speed took time to achieve but soon both boys were moving at a greater speed. Bray kept his eye on the artefact as he bounded along. He kept his

The Magic Portal

balance in check as just a slight miscalculation had him wobble off course. He had to bound harder to catch back up to Zac. His heart pumped. The time was ticking away as he kept calling out directional course to his companion.

Zac turned his head. 'It's in sight.'

'We have three minutes Zac. If you don't get it first go, we lose. Go faster.'

Bray felt flushed and sweat dripped inside his suit. Inside his helmet his glasses were almost fogged up but he squinted to read directions and pushed hard. Not until they were pulled out would either give up.

He saw Zac make a dive for something and hoped it was the artefact. He shook his head, and the sweat ran down his glasses giving him blurred vision. Zac's legs were longer and he had made it, but was falling with it to the surface. The power in his boots had been used up. He saw Zac struggle to get out the disc. He wasn't sure if he got it but heard him yell, 'Push the red button.'

Bray had to trust he wasn't just freaking out. Bray went to flip the cover and pressed the button, but his own shoes ran out of power. It flipped him over and in a spin he was powerless to do a thing. There was also no way he would reach Zac because he was spiralling out of control. Down, down, down he fell, heavily towards the surface. Had he pressed the button? And if he did, had Helios received it? If he didn't press it, they were both going to hit the surface gasses and be sucked into Jupiter's core.

Screaming as he got close, he had no idea where Zac was and could no longer hear his cries for help. Suddenly he was whisked up in a tornado-style wind tunnel that crackled with electric coloured lights, similar to laser lighting. It was beautiful and in it he looked for his buddy but Zac was nowhere to be seen. Was this death? Had Jupiter's crust swallowed him up and this was the inner heart of the planet? His heart slumped in sadness as he feared he didn't send out the call to Helios.

Chapter Sixteen

Suddenly Bray was thrown free and landed on soft ground with a splash. It was muddy and slushy.

'Where have you been?'

He heard a voice and swung his head around. Zac sat on a rock. He looked as if he had been crying.

'I was so worried, so glad you're okay Zac. You disappeared. I was thinking the worst. You are all right aren't you?'

'I saw you falling above me but I was picked up and brought here first. I've been sitting here waiting for twenty minutes. Geez, I thought you were dead.'

'Same. Wow that was close. We better work smarter on this one.' Bray got up and put an arm around Zac. 'Sure you're okay?'

Zac smiled. 'Yep, I now trust Helios knows what he's doing.' He lifted his head to look at Bray. 'Hey! And did you see all the colours. What was that about?'

Bray removed his arm so Zac could stand up. 'We were close to the north pole. I guess it was Jupiter's aurora. The colourful array of lights are said to be a massive display. We must have been taken through them.'

Zac dusted the dirt from his spacesuit. 'Thought it was Helios using his magic to calm me down.' He shrugged. 'Whatever, it worked. And now we're both here, guess we can get moving on this planet. Though I have no idea where we are. I've searched for landmarks but can't figure out where he has dumped us.'

'In the mud.' Rotten sod. Bray was still wet and the mud stuck to him.

Zac grinned at him. He was so into Bray's new stepdad. He was such a prankster and this mud... had his fingerprints all over it. As far as the eye could see, there was no other water to be found. Helios would surely be laughing right now. He did, however, hope Bray and Helios would work it out for his mum's sake, and for his. Zac looked forward to a future with the addition of this god.

Even saying it gave him chills of excitement... *a god.* 'So what next?' He dusted off his pants that had dried in the wind while he waited.' In his hand he held the disc he had retrieved from the last planet and he handed it to Bray with a big goofy smile. 'Jupiter... done!'

Bray took the disc and wrapped his arms around Zac in a wrestling hold. 'You are my hero!' He squeezed him and laughed.

'Okay. Ouch.' Zac wiggled out of his grip. He knew he was just excited but he didn't live with an affectionate family like Bray. 'No need to touch the merchandise.'

Bray let him go. 'Sorry buddy. This is so exciting. We got the first one... tick!' He held up the disc and jumped around excitedly and kissed it. 'Jupiter didn't win... we won... we won.'

Zac agreed. 'Yes we sure did.'

Bray settled and reached in his backpack and pulled out two bottles of cold water and two chocolate bars. 'We deserve a treat.' He tossed one of each to Zac who ripped open the chocolate treat and stuffed the whole bar in his mouth. Bray grinned and tossed him his chocolate bar too. 'I'm sure you've got hollow legs. Here, have mine, you deserve it for not giving up. Even when your shoes stopped working you kept your eye on the prize.

You must really trust Helios.'

'I do. Well, I sort-of second-guessed my loyalty when you didn't show up straight away. But all good now.' He started to unwrap the second chocolate bar and just before putting it in his mouth, he pointed to it. 'Are you sure?'

Bray nodded. 'Sure, have it.' He'd sat down and was more interested in studying the NAVscan as he sipped his water. 'Here we are.' He held it up so Zac could see too. 'This blue light flashing here is the artefact.'

Feeling better Zac went over and sat on the boulder next to Bray. 'But this isn't Saturn.' He pointed at the screen, then pointed up. 'That is Saturn.'

Bray had been so focused at being landed in mud he hadn't realised they weren't nestled inside Saturn's rings of water ice and rocky material. His feet sank into sand. The atmospheric orange haze gave the surface a ghostly weirdness. 'The NAVscan indicates we're in the desert. Where I landed before is a dried up river bed.'

Zac kicked at the mud. 'Maybe this sludge isn't of Helios's doing after all, but an underground river that has sprung up naturally.'

Bray grinned. 'He's back on my Christmas list then.'

Zac crossed his arms. 'Not back on mine yet. That was scary being here alone. He's still in the naughty corner for bringing you the long way here.'

The weather must have been icy cold because the wet mud had frozen into a high popsicle where it sprayed out of the ground.

Zac had followed Bray's fixed stare and was glad they were warm in their protected outfits that were made of some thin alien lightweight material. The helmets were so fine around the mouth they could easily talk. But that wasn't all that amazed him. He turned back to Bray for answers. 'How did the artefact land here? I thought it was on Saturn when you looked last. And where is here?'

'Just looking. I'll see if any messages have come through for us.' Bray said.

Zac studied the screen but wasn't sure what he was looking at. For the past few years Bray had studied ancient languages at school. It was the only class they didn't take together. Zac preferred modern languages. He was now fluent in Chinese, Greek, Italian, French and Japanese. However, this didn't help him read what popped up momentarily as Bray switched from screen to screen to see if any information had been sent by Helios.

'Ah here it is.' Bray looked relieved. 'Hey

what! We're on Titan. And this thick atmosphere is orange due to a dense nitrogen haze.'

'That's why I thought it was Saturn because of this orange glow around it.' Zac shrugged. 'Isn't Titan Saturn's biggest moon? In fact I read it was the second biggest of all moons and very similar to our planet… well, Earth in the early years of the ice ages anyway.'

Bray stood suddenly, his jaw dropped and eyes wide. He was getting a weak signal. 'Our artefact is on the move.' He screwed up his face as a different reading beeped on the screen. 'That surface break we landed on wasn't a game Helios was playing. It is where the artefact must have hit. Somehow it burrowed itself below the surface causing that flood of water. It may be on a stream floating under us…' He turned and pointed the NAVscan tracking it. 'You said Titan's a moon that's similar to Earth, only alien. There may be life here. What if one of these inhabitants has used magic to beam up our artefact?' Bray hoped he was wrong but all indications led to this revelation.

Zac pulled at his chin in thought. 'Bet whoever it is protects it as Witch Rhapsody tried to on Mercury.'

'A bit far-fetched Zac. But after the scheming that went on to prevent us getting Mercury's artefact, by the Erc and that witch, I guess anything is possible.'

A sound made them both look around. Behind them stood six weird orange-skinned aliens. Standing up high on their heads were brown feathers that resembled a Mohawk's head gear. The brown, black and tan feathers were softer around their bodies and covered all but their faces, hands and feet. They held up just one hand with three webbed fingers. Their feet were the same but huge like flippers. Amazingly, their faces were almost human to look at but with very fat cheeks and no external ears; just holes to hear. They made a sound that Zac noticed Bray strained to hear.

'Can you understand them?' said Zac. To him it sounded like a click clanking sound his granny made without her teeth.

Bray walked a step closer to them and pointed to the mud where he and Zac had splashed down a while ago. It must have been about the same time the artefact arrived to have it still muddy there.

The smaller one nodded and continued in the weird clack clunking language. He used his webbed paw to point in the direction the artefact was heading. So they knew something. This was the first time Zac wished he'd gone with ancient language, though surely Bray hadn't learned Titanian?

Bray turned to him. 'They're from a tribe called Ittans. It's hard to understand but I think they want to help us.'

'News of what we are trying to do must be spreading.' Zac puffed out his chest. 'Earth may never learn of this but at least up here we are becoming heroes.'

Bray put his hand up and chuckled. 'Don't get ahead of yourself buddy. I'm not even sure I have it right yet.'

'Well you don't need to Bray. Why wouldn't they want to help us? We know after our run in with the witch and Helios's kidnapping that many believe they will be reincarnated into a more perfect world. That's why they oppose our attempt at preventing the end of the universe. This tribe looks friendly and most likely do not believe in reincarnation, so they have come out of hiding to help.'

As if the spokesperson for the tribe understood he drew a picture in the sand.

Bray could understand better now they had pictures to go with the strange clicking dialect. 'Okay, so they live underground in caves. But it looks like recently an invader tribe from another world had made its presence felt and set up camp some distance from here. My guess he is saying three miles away. Oh and guess what the invaders' tribe is called.' Bray pulled a face.

'You're kidding... Not those no-good, mind-blurring, evil, furry Ercs from Mercury.' Zac shook his head in disbelief.

'Yes. And they say the leader of this tribe is called ... you guessed it, Witch Rhapsody. If I have the drawing and dialect correct, she has threatened to remove their feathers, leave them naked and not allow them to be reborn into the new universe. Or something to that effect.'

'Yet they still want to help. Brave feathered men. Ask them if the witch, Rhapsody, is still here on Titan,' said Zac.

In their dialect Bray asked the question and, receiving a response, turned back to Zac. 'As you saw by that drawing in the sand, she's at the campsite now. Appeared a few hours ago. It's on the edge of the desert and that is where the Ercs are heading too. And if I have translated it correctly, they have our artefact.'

'What are they intending to do for us? Or are they here to watch?' asked Zac.

Bray grinned at his buddy's impatience. 'I'll try to move this along but it's not an easy language to translate.' Bray was enjoying at last using what he had learned about language development to decipher the sounds into words. Yet it was taking up valuable time. He asked the leader if he knew where the artefact was and could they help them get to it.

'What is he saying?' said Zac.

When the feathered man stopped talking Bray turned to Zac. 'The Ercs grabbed the artefact and escaped through a tunnel. They are currently traveling on land. However, these guys live beside a river that is the gateway to many other channels. Water is their natural habitat. They can swim faster than the Ercs can move so they believe they can get us to them before they reach their camp and the witch.'

Zac shrugged. 'What we waiting for?'

Bray nodded to the little one who had been their spokesperson and gestured for them to lead the way. Only they didn't move. Instead the surface begun to swallow them up as they sank deep down within it. Bray had only enough time to slip the NAVscan in his pocket and flip over the seal before being gobbled up by the sand. Closing his mouth he forgot he had the full face mask on because it was so light. He could still breathe and keep his eyes open as they slipped through the sand, but it was a scary sensation to fall and not know how long it would last.

Suddenly they exited out of the surface crust and now were free-falling towards water. They were in what he guessed was a huge underground cave. Once they reached water the Ittans dived in with elegant grace, and zero splash. Bray and Zac came down fast. Both grabbed their knees and did a bomb dive that sprayed water over others on the cave edge.

'That was the best one ever,' Bray spun around in the water and bragged to Zac.

He agreed with a 'whoop whoop! What a blast!' His first was in the air.

Bray was suitably impressed with the space outfit he wore. It kept him afloat, warm and dry. He wriggled in the water to stay facing Zac. 'What a blast. These dudes are amazing.'

'I know, right. Did you see the swan dives and not even a splash?'

Bray chuckled. 'The coolest way to get to the bottom of a cave I've ever seen. And look how they live.'

They both moved about splashing and making so much noise, they must have frightened some of the tribe members that were sleeping by the water's edge. They sat up, eyes like saucers.

'Sorry!' Bray tried to say in their language

but it was met with grunts so he figured he got it wrong.

Zac chuckled. 'Cool Bray. Real cool.'

Bray splashed him. 'Well you're no help.'

They both held hands over their mouths, muffling a laugh. 'Guess we better stop having so much fun and get moving or we will never catch the Ercs,' said Bray.

'Agree. But do these guys know we can't swim to save ourselves?' said Zac.

Bray smiled. 'Nope,' he said and kept smiling.

'What's amusing?' Zac dog paddled closer to him.

'Just thinking how we learned to keep afloat. First time I've ever been glad we met Grogan. I mean his bullying has given me the will to survive. It has made me fearless in this quest. All this is purely adventure and fun compared to the hurt, humiliation and pain we suffered in the hand of that bully.'

Zac nodded in agreement. He too felt alive, excited and full of guts as he settled and begun to tread water. He went quiet as he followed Bray's concentrated stare towards the other Ittan tribe members. He too noticed there were many levels to the cave before them. Some tribe members huddled up in pockets in the cave walls, sound asleep. Others sat by the water's edge and chatted in that strange dialect. 'Have you worked out what language it is Bray? That's if it *is* a language anyone on Earth would know?'

'The clicking clunking sounds had me tricked for a few minutes. Well, until I used our Morse Code to work out their alphabet. I took a punt and answered back using this theory and they got excited, so knew I was on the right track,' said Bray.

'I was gobsmacked you worked it out. You know you're a genius.' Zac pushed him under the water playfully.

Bray came up chuckling. 'Hello! That's why we are bullied, because we are geniuses.'

Zac was about to speak again when a few youngsters in the tribe pointed fingers and laughed.

'They think us mucking about is funny,' Bray told him.

'They're so primitive Bray. No beds. Their tools look homemade and they don't even have a fire burning to warm them. Bet they only use water as a means to hunt.'

Bray grinned. 'Well, I think we just showed them a game to play in water.'

'They can thank us later. Maybe they will call it Zacdunk,' Zac said, and chuckled.

Bray splashed him. 'Fool, as if.' Then his attention was on a couple of the tribespeople that came out from a cave. They reminded Bray of Native American Chiefs with unusually long feathers coming from the tops of their heads that ran all the way down their backs. These trailed behind them as they walked.

'Wow check those long-haired louts. They sure need a feather cut,' Bray whispered to Zac, who muffled a laugh.

'No use whispering. Firstly they don't understand us and secondly,' he said, shrugging, 'they just don't understand us. But seriously Bray, isn't this amazing to find life on another planet? Wish we had time to find out more about them. I'm having a blast on this moon... I mean Titan. Just wish we could slow this mission down a little. You know, feed our curiosity. Wonder if they have bullies up here.'

'Well the others haven't come back to get us yet and neither of us can swim that far so I guess we have plenty of time to check out the locals.' Bray lifted his brows. 'Did you notice they have feathers but no wings?'

'Yep, and webbed hands and feet like ducks,' said Zac.

The corners of Bray's mouth dropped. 'Poor things, they got half of one breed and half of another. Can swim but can't fly.'

Zac tapped his lip. 'That means they're warm-blooded like birds. The reason those ones sleeping have their feathers fluffed out is to keep warm.'

Bray nodded in agreement and just about to keep discussing it when he was interrupted by the others who popped up in front of him. He turned his head back to Zac. 'Looks like we're on the move again.'

Zac took one last look. 'We are so lucky getting to see this. Just feeling so pumped now. Ready when they are.'

The little one smiled and made sounds in a clacky-toothed grandpa tone. Zac figured him to be a tribe elder as he had grey feathers and wispy white fluff around his face. It made him look like a grandpa. He made the sounds so fast Zac blinked and shook his head. 'What! How can you decipher that?'

Bray grinned. 'I'm a genius remember.' He

started to wrap his arms around a bigger Ittan's neck. 'Grab a ride Zac. We have to leave now. Something to do with the current. It helps them move quicker. That's what they were waiting for, was the tide to roll out.'

Zac reached out to the feather man next to him. He kept still while Zac got comfortable.

Bray noticed his buddy's look of concern. 'It's okay, they can take ten times their weight and we can breathe anywhere in these masks, so we'll be fine under the water.'

No sooner had he finished speaking when the feather man he rode submerged. Once he stopped wriggling his ride dived down deep, taking only seconds to catch up to the others.

Zac could see Bray was fully enjoying this experience. Excited about their world he turned to Zac and pointed out unusual fish and critters. There was one that looked like a massive prawn with huge wings. It was so big, Zac ducked his head and hid his face in the feathers until he saw the shadow leave. Even though the plant life colours were beautiful, underwater was not his favourite place to be. Even at home he never swam in his pool in the back yard. He shuddered if his sister asked him to join her.

'Eeek.' He felt something disgusting running

along his back. He almost fell off as he moved to the side of the feather man to get away from it. He viewed it from the side and saw it had centipede legs on a fat body with a head twice the size of his body. It bared its teeth as it eyed Zac and licked its lips.

Luckily his ride saw Zac was being sized up for a snack and shot off in another direction to lose the predator. Twice it got close and snapped its teeth but his ride darted off in a zig zag motion. They hid in some bright orange reeds that camouflaged the orange feathered man, but not Zac. The thing spotted Zac and tried to enter the reeds. Its teeth snapped and snarled but as soon as it touched the reeds it dropped to the floor of the river. Its tongue hung out, and it looked paralysed.

The feather man motioned for his rider to get back on and with Zac secured swam off quickly. His huge feet acted as flippers and before long they had caught up with the others who had only just stopped.

There were a lot of hand signals and nodding going on between Bray and the little feather man. Together they all surfaced.

Zac had already figured out that it meant they had caught up to the Ercs.

'Hey Zac, where you been? Was just going

to send Trigger here to find you.' Bray pointed to the small feather man doing all the communicating.

Zac's body slumped and he shook his head. 'Was nearly something's dinner.'

'Cool. A story to tell me later.' Bray smiled and seemed at home with all the weirdness. 'They're going to take us up to the moon's surface now. The Ercs have stopped for a rest and most are sleeping. They think this will be our only chance to sneak in and snatch our artefact back. When I signal we have it, they'll bring us back down here to make our escape.'

Zac put his thumb up. 'Sounds like a plan. Let's show those evil-thieving Ercs us humans are not to be messed with.'

'I'm so liking this new Zac. Chased by a predator has fired you up buddy. Let's do this then before we lose our nerve.' Bray turned and let the helping party know they were ready to go upside. 'They said to hold on tight.'

Zac did as he was told and in a fluid motion his ride dived into the depths of water. On the way up, he gracefully sprang out of the water and as soon as his hand touched the cave roof, an opening appeared. It was much like a portal, which made Zac feel as if he was in a vacuum. It was similar to when the book sucked them into its vortex, but not as scary, most likely because they weren't going as far this time. In seconds he stood in the desert on Titan's surface.

Bray closed the gap with a friendly slap to Zac's back. 'Wasn't that the coolest thing we have ever done?' he whispered and muffled a chuckle.

'The scariest thing I've ever done. I think my undies need changing I packed it so bad when I was chased,' Zac remarked.

Bray barely held back laughter but controlled it after hearing a noise. With a sudden movement he put a finger to his lips, warning Zac to keep quiet. He squinted, his expression turned to serious and using eye contact he alerted Zac to the fact they were not alone. He whispered, 'The Ercs are just over the other side of this sand dune.'

Zac put a hand to his mouth and nodded. 'What's our plan?' he whispered back.

Bray shrugged. 'We're winging it. Let's take a peek.'

They both climbed the sand dune. When at the top they saw only two guarded the artefact they sought. The ancient box was still intact. It was obvious the Ercs had no clue how it opened.

'What are they arguing about?' Zac couldn't hear what was being said.

'It's something about the food they shared.' Bray watched on as one threw it away in a mood and when the other got up to get it, the cranky Erc went with him. While they picked it up and fought about it, Bray saw his chance. Turning to Zac he put his hand up to gesture for him to stay. He whispered close to his ear, 'If I get caught I'll need you to sneak in later and save me. Or go get the others. Although I wouldn't count on their help. They're scared of the witch. So we could be on our own.'

'What's the signal to get them to help?' said Zac.

Bray smiled. 'SOS... I picked it because I knew you would know what that would be in Morse Code.'

'Okay, but hurry. I don't like you going alone.' Zac wiggled back so he was out of sight.

'I know, but I'm smaller. Should be able to duck and hide behind that stuff that looks like tumbleweed. I'll use it to hide me until I get past those that are sleeping.'

'Good plan.' Zac looked happier upon understanding what Bray was thinking.

As soon as you see me with it in my hands, alert the Ittans and they will pull us both down under the surface.'

'Okie dokie.' He placed his hand on Bray's shoulder. 'Be careful.'

Bray nodded and ran off, sliding down the dune that luckily was not frozen solid, and glad the wind storms on Titan kept it loose.

So far so good. Bray slid into the tumbleweed and started rolling it, being careful to keep his body concealed. He was just about to put his hand on the artefact when a hand reached for it and picked it up. *Blow it.* He kept still.

'Wake up varmints. Time to move on,' the leader said, using telepathy.

Bray trembled. He had forgotten the way they communicated. He willed himself not to think so they didn't pick up his thoughts. But he forgot about Zac. He would have forgotten too.

'Up there!' The leader pointed towards Zac. 'We have a spy tracking us.'

Zac ducked and Bray heard him call out an SOS for help. Both boys were pulled underground.

Zac was upset. 'So sorry Bray.' He turned to him and saw Bray had the box. 'You got it? Oh man, I thought I stuffed that up.'

Bray grinned. 'I heard you start to send out the SOS so jumped out from behind the tumbleweed

Adventures of Bray and Zac

and screamed really loudly at the leader. Figured if they use telepathy he wouldn't be used to loud noises. I'm not sure if it was the noise or that I frightened the bejeezers out of him. But it did work. He fumbled the box in fright which gave me a chance to snatch it from him. Next thing, I'm here.'
Bray was being held out of the water by two strong hands while he sat on the feathered man's stomach. He spoke to Bray telling him he would keep his top half dry while he put the box somewhere safe. Bray tucked it in his backpack, suddenly realising it had actually stayed dry inside, though he and Zac had been in the water for some time getting to that spot.

The small feather man asked if they were ready to move. Bray zipped it up, slipped into the straps over his shoulders and put his thumbs up to let them know he was ready. It was as they began to move that he clicked to what had happened. The straps felt stronger and had a waxy feel to them. He screwed up his lips, finally getting that Helios had said he couldn't get involved yet had thought of everything. He'd obviously swapped Bray's bag with one of alien material. So far this mission, Bray hadn't really looked in his bag and he wondered what else Helios had slipped into it.

When they arrived back at the cave where the Ittans lived, Bray dialled in to Helios to let him know they were ready to leave. He then removed the disc from the artefact box and after clicking a photo of the writings on it, gave the box to his new friends for helping them.

He had only just handed the box over when both he and Zac were sucked into a portal of Helios's making.

They had now conquered the two giant gas planets. They had two more to go. These last two planets were described as giant ice planets, and this particular one both boys wanted to visit. It made them laugh every time it was mentioned.

Chapter Seventeen

Without warning both boys felt suspended in air. It was dark and they moved very slowly. Something hard pressed against their feet and they realised they were standing upright. A blinding light switched on that had them both cover their eyes.

Bray pressed in close to Zac. 'Where do you think we are? If this is the 42 years of darkness this planet is experiencing, then where is that light coming from?'

'Pull the secondary visor down,' said Zac.

Bray adjusted his visor on his helmet. 'I can see four marble pillars. The light's coming directly from above us. I can see movement coming from it.'

'Me too,' said Zac. 'This planet has life. I can see shapes moving to the tops of those pillars and are sitting in the chairs up there. They must be some kind of council or higher beings come to help.'

'Or send us on our way.' Bray chewed his lip nervously. Normally he'd be the one excited, but this seemed a bit too orchestrated. They could be manipulative beings and their magic must have been stronger than a god's or Helios would have put them miles away from here, *and them.*

The light above them split. One beam stayed on them and four beams now shone towards the aliens. Although they were almost translucent with the light on them, their golden robes with hoods showed they were human-shaped. Three of them had their robes open and their well-fitting white dresses with gold embroidery easily defined them as females. The male removed his cape and sat dressed in white shirt, gold vest and jacket. Now seemingly comfortable he leaned forward and spoke. 'You have already guessed we are the high council. The tall one has also thought our names and he is correct. We are rulers from the neighbouring moons and responsible for whom we allow here. I am King Oberon, and to my left is my queen, Titania. Opposite me is Lady Miranda and next to her, the sprite Ariel.'

'If you were kind rulers we would not be stuck to this floor.' Bray struggled to move his feet. 'You have no right to hold us here.'

The sprite, Ariel, giggled. 'He is a feisty one he is.'

'Bray, that last planet has your head scrambled still. Think about it, the winds up here are up to 900 kilometres an hour. I'm assuming they have us in a vice more for protection than to harm us. You're tired. Chill,' said Zac.

'The tall Earthling has his wits about him.' King Oberon spoke aloud.

'Unusual for this species. Especially so young.' Queen Titania now listened with interest.

Lady Miranda batted her long lashes. 'Hurry this along. Get them on their way so we can all get home. Foolish race.'

'Well this foolish race is trying to save your life!' Bray yelled at her. 'Now let us go do what we came here to do.'

Zac nudged him. 'Bray, stop it!' He whispered. 'We need their help now they've pulled us off course.'

Bray breathed out. 'Okay, you're right.' he shoulders slumped. 'It's this place. It gives me the creeps. The floor's yours.'

Lady Miranda sat forward and glared at them. 'What is this nonsense? It is you trying to save your own necks, you insolent Earth mites...'

She was interrupted by the king who put his hand up. 'Hush My Lady. Let the smart one speak. Have your say, wise youngster.'

'Thank you Your Majesty. We apologise for this intrusion but we are on a time schedule to save the universe. We came here in search of an artefact; a box with an ancient inscription. If you would permit us to retrieve it we can be on our way. We mean no harm and will never be returning.'

Suddenly the artefact box floated just out of reach. Bray made a grab for it, missed and Zac only just caught him.

He screwed up his face. 'Was worth a shot. I would have dialled us out of here.'

Zac shook his head. 'They can hear us think. Well the king can. He's not that stupid. He knows already. This is a game for him and is allowing us time to convince the others. So please!'

'I know... I get it. Gob up, brain dead.'

Zac gave a slight smile and inclined his head to acknowledge he was spot on. He could already tell he had the king on side, and guessed they would all have to agree or they would be leaving without one of the pieces to their puzzle.

'The box! You were able to dislodge it from the ground? Your magic is very strong.'

Sprite Ariel leaned over and looked down at the floating treasure. 'We took it from a witch. She tried to steal from us she did. Punishable crime in these parts. She told us you were coming. This was a weapon to save your world and we were all doomed. Is this true what she said? I want to hear from the feisty one... yes you, the feisty traveller.' Her words were serious but her voice light, airy and friendly.

Zac elbowed Bray. 'You're up. Don't blow it. She likes you,' he whispered.

Bray looked up at the sprite Ariel and smiled. He liked her too, but none of the others. 'Oh yes, and I know exactly the one you mean. You'd be speaking of the witch, Rhapsody. This is the third planet where we have encountered her sabotage. She thinks the gods will save her when the universe destroys itself...' he tapped his chin. 'Let's see... oh in just four days' time. She believes that the gods intend to move all who rule these worlds to the new universe. The one they intend to create once this one is gone. But they won't, because—'

Lady Miranda interrupted. 'You don't know that. I will not stand for this rubbish any longer. Your Majesty, please put a stop to this nonsense now. I insist.'

The king leaned forward. 'Why do you think they would not take their immortal kin with them to rule on in a new universe? Very arrogant of you to think such a thing young Earthling.'

Bray put his hands on his hips. 'Well, have they asked you to go yet? It's only four days away. Wouldn't you need time to pack up your royal cases and have a rendezvous place to meet them? I mean have they even called you to a meeting and alerted you to the fact or have you only just found out from the witch?'

'That's enough.' He stood up. 'We need to talk.' He slipped on his hooded robe, the others followed his movement and once they were entirely covered, the four of them vanished.

'Bray what have you just done? We'll never get the box off them now. They'll think there is something in it to save them alone.' Zac flopped down on his backside. Unable to move his feet he wrapped his arms around his knees. 'It's over.' He was almost in tears. 'Couldn't you have been a bit more diplomatic?'

'Zac, you know we have no time to dilly dally. I figure we've been here close to three hours. They have around seventeen plus hour days here compared with us so time is moving fast. We still have one more planet. I gave it a shot. Let's see if the shock I injected is enough to get them moving on an answer.' He patted his shoulder. 'Just give it a few minutes. Truth hurts but they are smart enough to see it is the truth. And if they don't get on board with this and help us, they are as the witch told them, doomed.'

Suddenly the light flashed and the four beams moved down to their platform. The four figures appeared before them. Their translucent faces came into view. Their eyes were focused on them and their stance was stubborn and regal. What they did next changed Bray's dislike towards them. He noticed first that Zac's feet were released and he stood up. Then Bray was able to lift one foot at a time and, impressed, he looked up. To have the council join them on the platform and trust them enough to set them free showed Bray they had become the good guys.

King Oberon crossed his arms. 'And two kids were chosen to save us all. What were they thinking? I could have crushed you with my mind being so mad at your outburst towards us. Yes my boy, the truth does hurt.'

Bray, mimicking the king's posture, folded his arms and put a cheeky grin on his face. 'Being "kids" as you put it, just kept us alive. I'd say we have proved why we were chosen.'

'Cheeky right to the end. I want your names and who picked this duo. No more dilly dallying as you put it.'

My name is Bray and this is my best mate Zac. Helios chose us.'

The king threw his head back and laughed heartily. 'He is my favourite of all gods and this is typical of him. To send a boy to do man's job. Why would he not come to me himself?' He rubbed his head, his brows pulled in tight with that thought.

'He is not allowed to interfere. We have had to save him and his son and hide them. Zac and I came up with a plan to use a decoy and use this one day to gather the final boxes before the gods catch on that we have what we need. After today we lie low. Keep out of sight until we make this thing that will prevent total universal annihilation.'

'Why will the other gods not help?' Lady Miranda spoke quite kindly.

'They will always live on. They are gods. They have the powers to create a newer and improved universe. They will start again. Take what has been learned and make it better.'

'Yet you, just a child, want to save us all.' Queen Titania gave him a grin.

Bray put his head down and shook it. When he looked up there was real emotion in his eyes. 'No, just my mum.'

The Magic Portal

The queen eyed Zac. 'And you?'

Zac for the first time ever put an arm around Bray. 'Just my best friend.'

King Oberon put his hands by his sides. 'Well that isn't the answer we were expecting. But it shows us loud and clear, you do not lie even to save yourselves.' He breathed out slowly. 'We have all we need to know. Our decision made. Your fate has now been decided.' The king nodded to the one person Bray had a few cross words with, Lady Miranda.

She pulled the artefact from under her cape and passed it to Bray. 'Then make your mother proud of her son. I too understand to look at the big picture is daunting. Scale it down to what is important. That pumps adrenalin into your body just from that one thought and that power will make any dream come true. You are already a hero; our hero.' Her voice cracked a little and her hand shook as he took the box from her.

Bray smiled. 'Coming from a heroine, that's cool.'

No sooner had Bray finished his last words than they were sucked up into a vacuum of air and into a vortex.

'Helios must have been watching,' Zac called out. 'Thanks Your Kingliness, ladies.' He saluted to the figures they left behind.

'Bye Sprite Ariel. Come visit me when I get older.' Bray waved, giving her a coy smile. Both boys' chuckles were cut off as they were swept into a portal...

Chapter Eighteen

Neptune

They fell through thin wispy clouds. Next passed through the rings they had seen from a distance and found they were layers of debris scattered in the atmosphere. A strange substance surrounded them and formed a protective sphere. They were looking out at each other through this bubble.

'Can you hear me?' called out Bray.

'Sure can,' Zac put two thumbs up.

'Helios gets a big star on his work for this invention.' Bray chatted as he got his footing and stood up. 'Let's see what these bubbles can do. Should be similar to those we had a go at on Earth last summer.'

'Yes but these aren't plastic and this ain't Earth.' Zac braced his hands of the sides gingerly, trying not to move too much.

'Come on Zac, our last planet. Let's have fun on this one. All we know is it's the last giant gas planet.'

'We are sinking fast into the atmosphere, about to fall into the water below us, Bray! You call this fun?'

'I know, come on buddy, it's Neptune the home of the sea god, Poseidon? It bet it is water and these bubbles are to get us to the ocean floor. That's where the Navscan is telling me to go... down there!' He pointed. 'Helios has given us a means to get there. Let's see how fast these bubbles move.'

'He could have given us a submarine. But if this is it I may as well quit bitching and start rolling this sucker. You lead, Bray. You know I've got your back, no matter what.'

'That's the spirit,' Bray grinned. 'Now if I remember correctly we just started running. Just pretend I just called you a girl... Girl!' Bray yelled out and started to run. At the same time he laughed at Zac's face that turned red at being called a name he hated most. He looked behind. It had worked. Zac was running behind him. Getting their footing they ran inside the bubbles making them speed up or slow down. Bray deliberately played chasey; he twisted and turned to help them both learn how

The Magic Portal

to control the transport they were given. Once he saw Zac begin to smile and his enjoyment became obvious, Bray headed for the water. By this time they were both confident and laughed heartily as they rolled side by side touching down into blue hydrogen-methane atmosphere. Finally, they submerged into the water. Deeper and deeper, they went as Bray held the NAVscan tracking the artefact that beeped below. They could both hear each better under the water. Without the maximum velocity winds and storms which at times made it almost impossible to hear, now they floated and rolled their bubbles quietly, side by side.

'It might be the smallest of the four gas giants but it's by far my favourite. That blue we just came through was unreal,' Bray said as he and Zac scampered like mice inside their bubbles.

Zac made a sideways move and bumped Bray who shot off in the opposite direction.

They were thrown way off course and had to work hard to join back up with each other and get back on target.

'Sorry!' Zac chuckled. 'I was concentrating on keeping up with you, scooter. All I did was look around. I only glanced for a second and was amazed at how clear and blue the water is.'

Bray was multi-tasking. He had his NAVscan

in one hand, using the back of that hand to keep his momentum. He grinned. 'Zac, you are so uncoordinated when it comes to sporty games.'

'Am not. I just got a surprise. Took my mind off what I was doing for a minute. Look! This is all I did.' He craned his neck and viewed the area. Once again he bounced into Bray and knocked them both off course for a second time. This time Bray gave Zac a nudge and bounced him deliberately away. It turned into a game that continued as the alien spheres easily travelled down under the water. Both were in hysterics as they had fun inside their crazy bubbles.

It was Zac who stopped first. He got serious. 'Hey maybe we'd better check where we are. You picked it up on the last planet about the time issues. It's even less time here. Helios is working on Earth time, a twenty-four-hour cycle. On Neptune, their cycle is approximately sixteen hours. So instead of having three hours here we have around two hours. With that in mind, we have used up as much time as we can spare learning to manoeuvre these bubbles.'

'Agree Zac, so stop mucking about. Get serious lad.' Bray sounded just like Helios. He took him off perfectly.

Zac broke up into a fit of laughter. 'You stop mucking around and making me laugh then.'

Suddenly it registered what Zac had said. Bray looked at his watch. 'Cripes, what happen to the time!' His eyes widened, his smile faded. He had popped the NAVscan in his pocket and quickly fumbled getting it out. Tapping on the screen he saw they had gone way off course. 'Grrrr,' he growled at his stupidity and tomfoolery. 'It's way back in that direction.' He pointed behind them and to the right. 'We went straight past it. But I'm not sure how much deeper it is so we better get a real wriggle on.'

Both boys took off like crazy people, legs running and arms and hands flailing around to maintain their balance and to give them a bit of extra speed. Both knew about the bends and going so deep started to worry them.

'Are you worried about decompression sickness?'

Zac saw the concerned look on Bray's face.

'Was thinking about it... you too?' said Bray.

'Well,' Zac glanced at Bray. ' Thinking about this logically we are in like a vacuum of some kind and we still have these masks on to breathe, right? So I'm almost positive we won't get the bends on our way back up to the surface. Also, it would have been Helios who put us in these things so I trust he knows what he's doing.'

'Hope you're right because it's too late now anyway, Look! We're nearly at the bottom!' Bray squealed with excitement.

'I can just see it. But how are we meant to get it inside this bubble?' Zac shared his concern.

Bray shrugged. 'Whatever we have to do,' he said as he looked at the watch that Ochimus had given him, 'we have ten minutes to decide. After that we run on Earth time and don't need to rush. You heard Helios. 'Ready or not he's pulling us out when the sun goes down.'

'So what you're saying, is that going by the NAVscan, in Neptune the sun goes down,' he checked his watch. 'In the next nine minutes.'

'Nope... eight minutes now. So if we are going to make a break out of these bubbles to snatch that artefact out of its box, we have to move it.'

'I'm ready then,' Zac said. 'So what's the plan? How do we get out?'

Bray had already thought of that and had taken off his backpack and was searching. All he found was an old plastic knife and no way was that going to work. 'Okay, one more thing left to try. He stood up and slung his backpack over his shoulder. 'We have to think it gone. Only way. If magic got us here, then magic can be dissolved with the will of the user's mind.'

'Seriously Bray. You believe that!'

Bray smiled. 'All I got. Now concentrate, Zac. We can still breathe underwater with these masks on, so don't let fear stop us finishing this together.'

'Together!' Zac slapped a hand on the wall of his bubble where it touched Bray's ball.

Bray did the same. If not for the thinness of the wall their hands would meet; in that exact spot the wall disappeared where their suit gloves met.

'That's it,' they both screamed at the same time.

Bray nodded. 'It melts away with the heat of our hands.'

Using this theory, they gradually rolled their bubbles, this time not pressing firmly against one another's hands. The melting of the substance joined the alien matter, and their bubbles, together.

'This time we don't quite touch Bray. Then we will make the opening on both our bubbles.'

They carefully rolled in sequence staying together but not quite connecting. Slowly the membrane of their bubbles broke down and their body heat melted away a big chunk of the membrane. Water rushed in which made it easier for them to swim out. Funnily enough it did not

Adventures of Bray and Zac

collapse, but they were out.

Once free they reached the bottom easily. The artefact was directly under them so it was easy to get at, but not so easy to pull from the ocean floor cavity. It was stuck as some of the others had been. This had been why many times they ended up with only the contents.

Zac unclipped the access panel and opened the artefact box and Bray reached in for the disc.

Zac didn't see if Bray had retrieved it before they were whisked away. Swirling, screaming and finally *thump!* they landed on hard floor. Helios, Ochimus and Bray's mum were looking down at them.

'Hell of a landing hey boys!' Ochimus knew how it felt, as it seemed he would have come back through it only seconds before.

'Did you get it?' Zac jumped up, staring at Bray.

Bray shook his head. His eyes were sombre and lip curled down. It didn't look good.

'We failed?' Zac screamed.

Bray shrugged and in a fast motion lifted up his hand. In it was the smallest of all the discs. 'We don't know how to fail. We're geeks!' He laughed.

The Magic Portal

Zac slung two arms around him and jumped up and down. 'We did it?'

'Yep, we did it buddy.' Bray bear-hugged him off the ground. 'You're the best buddy ever. Couldn't have done it without you.' He put him down.

Helios, Ochimus and Bray's mum had already started to celebrate together with a wine but excited put down their glasses to give the boys a hug.

'Well done lads!' Helios towered over them and with both huge hands ruffled their heads.

Ochimus jumped with the boys until they settled. 'Can't believe you little freaks did it. None of this could be seen. Even Father had no idea if you would complete this part of mission.'

'This was all you two. No help. I love you both so much,' Bray's mum held their faces in her hands and kissed them on the cheeks. 'My heroes.'

Bray pulled back. 'Hey, not so fast Mum. We still have to work out how to put this device together and the picture I took of the outer case is blurry.' He shook his head. 'That's because I snapped it as we got pulled into the vortex.' He held up the NAVscan to show her. 'See? It's out of focus. We're positive we need the markings to help us with part two of this mission.' His voice high as reality of the next task shook his emotions.

'Part two is the assembly.' Zac stopped celebrating and stood staring at the picture. 'Bray, I think I remember the smudged details. Sit with me and help fill in the blanks. We have good memories. We can do this. Okay.' He soothed the moment.

Bray slowly grinned. 'Together.' He tilted his head up to Zac.

'All the way.' Zac gave him his best toothy grin that made Bray's smile widen.

His trust in Zac was so strong the negative thoughts faded as fast as they surfaced.

Sitting at the computer they both worked tirelessly getting the pattern correct in the system. After transferring the images of the artefact boxes that had been scanned, they made a start on the formula.

Helios sat looking on in amazement. Their dedication and technical advancement was well above his kind. Bray's mother fitted into their world as such a calming influence, taking them food, watching at times and giving advice only when asked. They both responded to Madeline as if she was the number one person in their life and getting to know this duo, she was. Zac had made a home with Bray and his mother, apparently only going home to sleep. He had to admit he wished it was him they needed. But for now he couldn't interfere. This ancient weapon was their number one priority. There would be plenty of time after this was all over to get to know these highly intelligent lads.

Adventures of Bray and Zac

Chapter Nineteen

Searching the Sky

'Bray, wake up!' his mum called out from the kitchen.

Through the haze and drool running down on to the desk top, Bray sat up rubbing his eyes before straightening up his glasses. He smelt food and shook Zac. 'Mum's cooking.'

Zac sat up so quickly he whacked his head on the desk light. 'Ouch.' He rubbed it as Bray's mum sat a huge plate of bacon, eggs, hash browns and their favourite, chicken sausages with her special spicy tomato sauce, in front of them.

'Thanks Mum. Looks delish.' Bray started shovelling food into his mouth.

'Yum, I second that.' Zac gave her a big smile.

She tousled his hair. 'You like anything.

Adventures of Bray and Zac

You're a good boy Zac. But my other son, well we both know he has picky tastebuds.'

That made Zac's smile widen. He liked it when she referred to him as one of her sons. He had always been made to feel one of the family. A deep emotion came over him. Not once in these past few days did he even give his family a passing thought. He wondered, only for a moment, if they missed him. Or would they be so busy as usual, they had not noticed he wasn't around much? He retraced his steps when he ducked home the day before to retrieve something from his room. Nothing had been touched and there was not even a note for chores. He had shrugged and left. Back to his adopted family. Back to where he was so happy his heart beat with a purposeful strum. Like now as his second mum gave him a hug, and she didn't need a reason.

'You lads have been up most of the night.' Helios pulled up a stool and balanced his food on his lap so he could eat and chat. 'Have you worked it out yet?'

'We have but there is a problem.'

'Always is.' He smiled. 'Can I help?'

'Not sure unless you can control the moon.' Bray put his fork and knife down. 'You see the alien discs are to be set in sequence under the light of a full moon. The direct glow of moonlight has to hit all eight of them at exactly eight o'clock for the molecules to activate.'

'And the problem is?' Helios said.

'Tonight is the eighth day, and we cannot wait any longer. It has to happen. But this evening there is no moon. The lunar cycle has ended and it will be moonless tonight.' Bray pushed his plate towards Zac, who always finished off his leftovers.

'Then we set it off from another planet. There will be many full moons to choose from,' Helios said with a wave of his hand, dismissing it as a problem.

'No can do. It has to be set off from Earth.' Bray turned to him, seriousness in his tone. 'The timing, the angle it must hit, the whole geometrics screams Earth. Nowhere else will work. We have run over a hundred simulations.'

'Oh dear.' Bray's mum looked horrified.

'Mum please don't be sad,' said Bray. 'We haven't given up and we won't until the end. I promise we will find way. After Zac finishes eating we're going to search for another light that will give the same output as moon glow. We've looked at everything from shimmering them under water like you do with gems, to using a specific filtered light. As yet nothing has worked, but the day's not over.'

'Well, it's midday. You have exactly eight hours, lads,' Helios said.

'Okay, I've finished.' Zac pushed his plate away. 'You guys just have to trust us. Bray will now search Earthly phenomena and I'm searching the skies for a meteor or something similar to give us light and heat.'

'Good... I feel better knowing you're not giving up.' Helios stood up. 'I'm not either but I have to make my own plans to save the sun if something goes wrong. It's part of me and if it goes I'll have no place in the old, or the new, universe.' He motioned towards Ochimus. 'Coming son? This involves you too.'

They went to the lounge where Helios had used his magic to set up a palace-like room. It was complete with two golden carved thrones for him and his son. It had Greek pillars, a huge bath, servants and lesser golden carved seating surrounding him. On these chairs sat the god's loyal council with whom he conferred, debated and argued for many hours of the day and night. Bray and Zac had gone in for a stickybeak a couple of days ago, but found it very old school and centuries behind them. They got bored within the first few minutes as they discussed matters at hand without using any research. Old fashioned robes and views and stagnant thinking kept the issues going around in circles. So when Helios and his son left the room they both grinned.

'Bet there will be no plans made in that room today. Well, not unless lateral thinking changes dramatically.' Zac chuckled.

Bray winked. 'Ready to get back to it?'

'Sure am. If we leave it up to them in there to come up with an idea to help us, we'll be waiting a few years,' Zac said.

'Few thousand centuries.' Bray smirked.

Chapter Twenty

Dark Matter

Bray and Zac chose to set off the alien device where they found the Earth artefact. This time as they laid out the discs on mother Earth's richest foundation, Grogan and his mates were nowhere to be seen. Helios, his parliament and council members, along with his royal guards were here to protect the weapon and give it every opportunity to work its magic. Helios believed so strongly in Bray and Zac, tonight he risked his position in the heavens to support the human race.

'Zac, they have to be in sequence. Can you check the order I've laid them in and double check that I have used the correct discs.'

Zac picked them up, one at a time, studied each and placed it down. 'Check Mercury.' He laid it down. 'Check Venus.' He placed it back in its spot. 'Check Earth...' He continued to call them out. 'Check Mars, check Jupiter, check Saturn, check Uranus and last, check Neptune.' He placed it down on to the rich soil.

Both looked up into the sky. Zac put his arm around Bray. 'We found it together, we were meant to finish this together. We've both given this our all and by sheer persistence and our geekiness, found the answer.'

'Great joint effort.' Bray put his hand up and Zac gripped it, squeezing hard.

'This will work Bray. I know it will. We deciphered every artefact box. And we worked out the last one.'

Neither worried their genius had missed anything. There was no time to change, rearrange or take time to come up with a plan B. They had made the call. The moment was now.

Suddenly there was a bright light followed by an explosion. Broken debris burst into flames and hurtled towards them.

'The meteor is heading this way Bray, just like we predicted.' Helios put his arm around them both. 'It's as life has always been, and will be, forevermore lads. It's now up to Mother Nature and the wonders in the universe to keep mankind alive. You've done everything that's humanly possible, used every ounce of energy and intellect to make sure this device has the best chance of

The Magic Portal

working this miracle. You even went as far as making sure the pieces are laid on this rich soil to give it extra power. That by the way, was pure genius.' He patted their backs. 'The rest of it is out of your hands and up to fate and faith. Stand back and let this extraordinary event finish what you have put your hearts and souls into. As for blast off, I have no idea how much energy this joining of supernatural power will need. Because of this you have to come with me to a safe distance. We want you two to stay alive to enjoy this universe you will one day leave as a legacy.'

He steered them to stand with Bray's mother. Fingers spread, he moved his hand slowly and put a ring of protection not only around them, but around his entire entourage and royal guards. A golden glow settled around them; the haze he knew would prevent clear vision but would stop any of them from being sucked up into the device of massive power.

'So very proud of you lads.' Helios's voice cracked as the emotion of the moment and the anticipation hit him. Even if this did not work, though the lads were solid and sure it would, he couldn't have felt more pleased with his choice of humans. He would never forget this moment and the fresh hopeful glow that he saw on Zac and Bray's innocent faces. It made his decision to help this primitive race worthwhile.

The large chunk of meteorite still on fire sped towards the discs that began to illuminate. The shower of burning rocks trailed behind the large portion. The light illuminated the discs. They lit up one after the other, so bright the spectators all shaded their eyes. But even the blinding glow didn't stop any of them from witnessing this miracle.

'It's reacting to it!' said Bray. 'Zac, we did it.'

Zac's smile was from ear to ear. 'It's as we thought Bray, the discs are starting to distort as if being welded, the sparks and hot liquid is starting to form the shape of a rocket.'

'Heaps cooler than the way Transformers shape into robots,' said Bray.

'Way cooler.' Zac's jaw was wide with amazement.

'Can't believe you boys picked this meteor up.' Bray's mum moved in between them holding each of their hands. 'It's working isn't it?'

Bray leaned into her. 'Yes, Mum. Did you ever doubt us?'

She squeezed their hands. 'I've been lucky enough to watch you both grow and develop a skill I never dreamed you would need. Feared for your lives, yes. But never a doubt in my mind that my boys were the only ones who could have pulled this massive task off.'

'Awe thanks Mum B.' Zac leaned into her.

'I wish your parents could have been here to share this moment with us,' Madeline said.

Suddenly came a screech of tyres and Zac's head spun around. It was Grogan getting out of a taxi. Zac's mum and dad were next to step out. Zac's focus went straight to Helios. He was worried Helios may be cross that not only his parents, but Grogan would now be aware of Helios's power and know about what they had been doing.

Helios shrugged.

'I told you they would be here!' called out Grogan as he pointed at them.

Zac's parents ran to him. 'You've been missing. We searched all over for you. An hour ago your friend Grogan came to us with the weirdest of tales. Said you and Bray would be saving the world tonight. We had to come. We didn't believe him but didn't know where else to look. Are you okay?' Zac's mum hung on tightly to his arm.

'Zac is there any truth to what Grogan has told us? Or is this some strange sect you have joined?' His dad's eyes were wide and still in disbelief of the scene they were witnessing.

'See!' Grogan pointed. 'Check out the old fashioned dude with the robe on. That's Helios. I'm right aren't I Zac?'

Helios put his hand up. 'There will be time to explain. But this is Zac and Bray's moment. Stay or go, but be quiet. Let them enjoy what they have risked their lives to complete for us all.' His voice bellowed, causing their words to snap off and there was silence. But not for long. Suddenly the air was thick with smoke and the sound deafening as a large chunk of meteoroid whistled past.

Zac's dad took a step closer and both parents now stood protectively beside their son. His dad put an arm around his shoulders, his mum holding on tightly to the other side of him. Zac smiled. Big and bright. He had won tonight in more ways than one. He felt complete as he watched the pieces they had collected come to life. Shards of the shiny disc opened like legs of a robotic spider, running and jumping one on top of the other. The alien hot liquid weaved together and formed a spine that continued to grow and twist. There were serious sounds of grinding and cogs turning and locking into place before it stood before them; a weapon taller than a five storey building. The biggest missile the humans standing there had ever seen up close. Then everything stopped. Cheers from them cut off and they stood in silence.

'What now?' Helios swung his head towards

the lads. 'I thought it would set itself off. Don't tell me we did all this for nothing. I can't believe it wants more blood.'

Zac shook free of his parents. 'You thinking what I am Bray?'

'Sure am.' Bray turned to Grogan. 'The pocket knife you always carry with you.' He snapped his fingers with impatience. 'I need it now!'

Grogan removed it from his pocket and looked pleased he could help. As he handed it over he smiled. It was the first time Bray had ever got a smile from him and gave him a grin in return.

'Anything for my boys,' said Grogan.

Without a word Bray and Zac ran to the weapon. As if it knew what came next, a little door slid open and out slid a vial. Bray opened the pocket knife and made a small nick at the top of his finger. Zac did the same and together they held their blood dripping fingers over the vial. It filled up quickly with the combination of their DNA. That was what it needed and both worked it out at the same time. It made sense it would need their DNA to imprint on the weapon and give it life. Their life. The vial disappeared and once the door slid shut the weapon began to shudder and shake.

This time Helios didn't go to them; he used his power to move them back to him. They were slid on heels, dragged away fast from the danger zone and back within his protection.

Helios shook his head and smiled. 'The final key to give it life. Well done lads.'

Cheers raised the vibration of the moment as the weapon powered up and shot off. Helios once again used magic and stretched out both arms. Above them an image of what was happening way out in the universe played out before them. It was so close they could have touched the image. From the ground they saw the direct hit of their weapon. They all wondered if it had worked. They waited as the dark matter seemed to angrily form around the missile. They all held their breath. Bray grabbed for his mum's hand and held it tight.

'Mum!' He looked up at her, worried.

'Have faith sweetheart.' She smiled. 'This will work because you don't know how to fail. Now look!' She saw it first. And there, way inside the blackness, he could see a tiny light, so small at first, they all squinted to see. Bigger and brighter it grew as bit by bit, the dark matter looked as if it was being chewed up. The device churned and devoured the blackness. It went in and came out the bottom in a cloud. The sparkling iridescent rainbow of colours streamed behind the weapon, so pretty they stood in awe. Eventually the darkness faded and brilliant reds, orange, gold and pink

The Magic Portal

flamed the space where only darkness had been. Stars shone out; a new galaxy had been created.

Helios looked up. 'We shall call this new galaxy...'

Within that split second, Bray, Zac and Grogan all jumped in the air and pumped their fists. 'Geeks rule,' they yelled together.

Helios shook his head. 'We will see.' He put up his hands and ended the image.

Cheers rang out as they jumped around hugging each and congratulated the boys. It was quite a moment, one none of them would ever forget.

After they calmed down it was time to go home. Sleep was something none of them thought of, but a nice cold drink of soda and heaps of chocolate was the request of the heroes.

Helios smiled at Bray and his mum. 'Am I coming home with you both tonight? I hope these hugs mean I'm forgiven.'

Bray's mum gave him a loving smile. 'Yes you are forgiven. I was hoping you would stay married to me.' She put her hand out and he took it, kissed it and looked at Bray. 'And you young man. Am I welcome?'

'I would love that, but I know how much you love your son. Thought after this was over you might go home to your old life. What will happen with Ochimus?' said Bray.

'Ochimus is my son, your new stepbrother and he will come to stay with us from time to time. But he's much older than you and he wants to take over the family business caring for the sun. This is good news for me. Now he has joined me in the business I will get to see Ochimus daily in the council chambers.'

'So that's where you went every day while I was at school?' Bray grinned.

'You see, we already know this arrangement works only I hope you will allow me into your life a little more now you know me better.'

Bray chuckled. 'I'll try not to slam the car door as hard. Wonder you didn't use your magic and put a silencer on it,' he joked.

'I did, on my ears.' Helios bellowed out a laugh.

Bray smiled at Ochimus with a shy quirk of his head now he knew they were going to be stepbrothers. He had always wished for a brother. 'What about you, Ochimus. Are you okay with your dad living here?'

Ochimus stepped forward. 'My father's home is on the island of Rhodes in Greece. Has been since it was founded. As a god, my father must keep his seat at the head of council. However, he has made it clear to me and our council, that if you accept him as your stepfather he will relinquish all he rules to my care.'

'Including the chariot?' Bray asked.

'Yes. Including the chariot and his horses Pyrios, Aeos, Aethon and Phlegon.'

'Wow!' Bray eyed Helios. 'You'd give it up for my mum? Seriously?'

Helios shook his head. 'You... and your mother. I want you both. I want a normal life with the two people in this world I have grown to love. I want to watch you grow and share with you wisdoms from my time.'

Bray put up his hand for him to stop. 'Okay,' he grinned. 'Not sure about your old ways but would sure love you to stay. But there is someone else who is a big part of our family that you have to get approval from.' He turned to Zac. 'What do you reckon buddy. Can you handle Helios as well as me and my mum in your life?'

'Wahoo!' Zac jumped and fisted the air. 'Sure could. A god in the neighbourhood. How cool.'

Ochimus put his hand up. 'No boys. Helios will be plain old Eishol. No magic. He will have to take away your memories of him as Helios. The gods would never allow him to be exposed like that.'

'But if I lose my memory, I might go back to disliking him again. I mean, I thought we would keep our memories of what Zac and I did. How can you take our adventure away? It's not fair!'

'No... it's not fair. That part was never mentioned to either of us!' Zac piped up.

'If you want my father in your family, they are the conditions or he has to leave for good. Not sure why he wants to stay here and not come home to his real place. But he's in love, which is plain to see. And as for you two, you have him twisted around your little fingers. But that's his call.'

Grogan spoke up from behind them. Until then he was too gobsmacked to say a word. 'He wants to stay 'cause you're a jerk Ochimus. Can't believe you want all this erased. They just saved the universe and this is the thanks they get.'

'And who are you?' Ochimus bellowed.

Grogan could tell he was Helios's son. Not only did they look alike, but he commanded respect as his father had. Still they did not scare him. Neither of them did. He stood tall. 'I'm Grogan and those heroes are my best mates.' He went right up to Ochimus's face and glared.

'About time you stood up for the right thing mate,' Ochimus said. 'You have allowed your intellect to dwindle. You should have been a part of this but you let your anger guide you. There were a few situations they may not have needed to struggle so much if you had been with them. So this is your wake-up call. Get back on the path you should be on. And if I ever find you have bullied them or allowed them to be bullied, I will be back to teach you a lesson.' He turned and smiled at the boys then back at Grogan. 'Take care of them both, Grogan my boy, 'cause I for one will miss them.' He took a step towards Bray and Zac. 'Sorry you must forget all this, but it is our law to keep life on the planets secret. You both did a great job. Many will sing your praises and as for me, I consider you both my brothers, regardless of what happens here tonight with Helios.' He shook both of their hands, then faced Bray. 'So does Father stay, or come with us? Mind you, if he comes, he'll be miserable and a pain to live because he'll fret so much for you and your mum.' Ochimus smiled.

'He stays!' Yelled Bray and Zac.

Both smiled widely at Ochimus.

'Goodbye Father. I'll look forward to our next council meeting. Till then I promise to do you proud.' Ochimus hugged his father and waved farewell.

'I will miss you every moment until then.' Helios smiled back as his son, entourage, council and royal guards snapped out of sight.

Helios knelt and pulled Bray and Zac in for a hug. 'My young and noble lads. How I look forward to the years ahead. Thank you for giving so much of yourselves to this quest. Your dedication and loyalty for this day will be paid back in time. But for now, it's a school night and you need sleep. He ruffled his fingers through their hair and his magic made them fall instantly asleep. Two exhausted boys collapsed in his arms. They looked younger than twelve as they slept.

Helios put Zac in a taxi with his parents and Grogan. A bright light enclosed the vehicle as it drove away. He made sure that in the morning, no memories would be held of this night.

At home, Eishol stood over and watched his brave new son until his mother came to get him.

'Bray will love you. Give him time.'

'I know. I know,' Eishol shook his head and closed the door behind him. All human memories had to be wiped. It was just them again, as before. And he couldn't have been happier. It was past midnight and the universe was quiet. The weapon had worked. Helios grinned. It was the first day of the rest of their lives together and he looked forward to driving his hot-headed new son, and his toothy mate, to school in the morning. He couldn't wipe the excited smile from his face.

Bray and Zac thank you for coming along on their space adventure.

Hope you enjoyed your time in the solar system.

Look forward to you joining us on our next adventure!

Bye for now.

Bray & Zac

Information on the planets was sourced from the following website.

https://solarsystem.nasa.gov/kids/

www.ingramcontent.com/pod-product-compliance
Lightning Source LLC
Chambersburg PA
CBHW020645300426
44112CB00007B/251